MW01290601

ORION COUNCIL, HERE

KRISTA RAISA

with Katherine Hilaire

Copyright © 2014

by

Krista A. Raisa

All Rights Reserved. No part of this book may be used or reproduced in any manner without written permission from the author.

E-mail: kristaraisa@gmail.com

Website: www.GalacticFaery.com

Cover Design and artwork: Krista Raisa

Photos by Krista Raisa and Patrick Hilaire Photography

First edition. Printed in the USA

~Dedicated to all Starseeds and Elementals on the planet~

ACKNOWLEDGEMENTS

First and foremost, I thank my mother Katherine Hilaire, for co-editing this book. She is responsible for bringing forth the material in Part One, by asking the right questions. It was her love, courage, patience and wisdom, that helped me in creating not only my spiritual business, but my entire, vibrant life. Bless you, Mom: I am grateful for our countless nights of philosophy, healing and channeling.

I am most grateful to my father Ari-Tapani Räisä, for supporting my goals no matter what the subject. Isi, your presence has always propelled me forward, helping me maintain a healthy body and mind. You got me to Finland and back. I love you. Thank you for teaching me about angels, even with your scientific approach to "all things great and small."

To my step-parents Patrick Hilaire and Valarie Hing, who have taught me to love what I do and always consider others: thank you so much for your love and showering me with abundance. To my brother Kier who brings so much joy, laughter and music to my life: I love you and your creative, dancing spirit. Thank you for embracing me every time I come home, "Little Bear." You are a blessing to this world.

I want to give all my love and affection to my family, in Heaven and on Earth.

Thank you for your guidance and unconditional love: Tapani Räisä, Pirjo Räisä, Valerie Leiman, David Leiman, Albert Brown, Nancy Wolcott, Lilas Knight, Florence

Hazard, Paul Brown, Mirka Räisä, Kari Lampinen, Karoliina Lampinen, Joel Lampinen, the Torvinen family, the LaNear family, the Hilaire and Hing families, and my god-parents Eeva-Liisa and Saku Säisä, Pedro, Sandra, "Petsu" and Maisa.

This is only the beginning Rene Swain, a.k.a. my beloved Arcturus Ra. Thank you for uniting me with galactic family once again. I cannot wait to see what the future has to offer us. Your unconditional love and help continue to bring magic into this world.

In my heart will always be the Gamma Gamma Gamma Girls: Laura Vornanen, Pirita Härkisaari, Anna Pentikäinen, Tanja Blom, Elli Homanen, Henni Virtanen, Laura Kujala, Henna Pentikäinen, Aino Hietala, Saara Salmela. Also, thanks to my best friends: Henriikka Iivonen, Eveliina Kauppinen, Elina Lassila, "Hansu" Hellman, Riina Silvo, Aku Konttinen, Alice Jasper, Giselle Khan. Special thanks goes to those who supported me behind-the-scenes, for whom I am forever grateful: Janne and Ritva Hakkarainen, Eija Anderson, Timo Ylönen, "Witchy Wendy," Heidi Pekonen, and the Sedona star-tribe — you know who you are.

Finally, many thanks and much appreciation to the wonderful clients who have accelerated this work and helped to make it possible.

CONTENTS

AFTERWORD

INTRODUCTION

What is now in your hands or on your computer screen is a book of light. There are certain frequencies in this book that will bring light into your life and they will simply be felt. There is so much to life that is unexplained – unseen worlds, psychic visions, telepathic communication – and channeling is just one way of translating this non-physical energy.

Ever since I was a little girl, I was open to the idea that there is a Spirit World and I always felt safe and protected when thinking about it. I believe it is love energy that we feel when we allow ourselves to become instruments of the Divine and open our channels, although society often tells us that this is "bad," "weird," or "crazy." There are challenges and seemingly negative entities in the non-physical but everything that happens to us works by the Law of Attraction or has been put on our path as a test for our soul's development. The challenge is how we deal with situations that come our way. Personally, I have had several of these tests. Just because many people channel does not mean that they are God's favorites or have all obstacles removed from their lives.

Channeling is just one form of translating unseen energy and there are many ways to do it. I call my method "in-body channeling" which is similar to trance channeling but is more of a conscious flow of information; I am aware during my sessions.

Some channels have even experienced severe problems such as alcoholism and suicidal thoughts. However, this is part of the old paradigm which is falling away. The third dimension is crumbling. We are moving into a fifth dimensional frequency, becoming more aware of who we are and remembering our innate abilities. These include clairvoyance, clairsentience, clairaudience, telepathy, telekinesis, teleportation, empathy and all modes of healing, but the most important ability is our ability to love. We are bringing an energetic current of love to Earth that has never been experienced here before. It is the energy of Oneness that the High Council of Orion talks about: the Unity Consciousness that we feel and know in our hearts. For that reason, every single person on the planet is extremely important.

You may be an executive, a construction worker, teacher, retired, on a disability check or in high school, but your essence is that of Spirit. We are beginning to know this in our hearts and to realize that most of our lives have been what the Orion Council calls "programs." For many, this is upsetting because they believed that their purpose in life was to get a job, get money, get married and be "a success." Many have forgotten the contracts that their souls made prior to incarnating such as vowing to protect the Spirit of Earth (Gaia) or helping to awaken those who had "fallen asleep" in this time of mass remembrance.

If you are reading this book, you are in the process of remembering. The sessions in Part I were held in 2011 in which I channeled the Council of Orion, Archangels and other benevolent Beings of Light, while my mother, Katherine, asked questions of them. Part II is information received working with my clients through 2012. It is my hope that this book will both help you to better understand channeling and to know why you are so important to this world.

Blessings,

Krista Raisa

Sedona, AZ 2013

INTRODUCTION

It took a lot of courage for my daughter, Krista, to risk ridicule and go public with her channeling gift. Although she had several bouts of self doubt along the way, she bravely persevered and I truly admire her for it. It is true that not everyone is prepared to accept such an experience and I must confess that although I have witnessed many channeling sessions in the past, I was unprepared for experiencing it under my own roof, with my own daughter. Feeling protective of her was my instinctive response, however once the loving intent and high caliber discourse of the Council of Orion became apparent, I gradually relaxed into trust.

Many people express interest in learning to channel and on many occasions, the Council has stated that everyone is capable of developing the skill, yet they caution, "There is much to be learned." It is not to be entered into lightly or just for entertainment: intent is everything. Those seeking "fun and games" attract those unseen energies that are happy to oblige. There is also the matter of discomfort as the entire body adjusts. In many instances, our sessions together were interrupted or cut short due to Krista's overwhelming fatigue. Although the demands made upon her were considerable, few experiences can compare to having such conversations.

Aside from being, as the Council once teased, "a mother hen," I tried to ask questions that would be of interest to many different people and yet the book is quite personal. It reflects our early steps on the path of Ascension. For those of you who intend to have private sessions with Krista, I am certain that you will find the insights, perspectives, guidance and love from the Council and Archangels, to be deeply affecting on all levels.

Blessings,

Katherine Hilaire

New York, 2013

Orion Council, here. Good question, friend. Good question to know who is on the other end of the line. We are the Council of Orion. Hello. We are in many places but we come from the Central Sun. We are etheric at times but we originate in the solar system where creation happens. We are not human. We are energy Light Beings. We create. Many are working with us at this time. You see, friend, when you are traveling from other spheres of existence, the names are quite interesting. When you are traveling to the planet Earth, you need to have a name for humanity. Orion energy originates where we reside but we have many helpers at this time. Of course, you know Creator created many different planets in your galaxy, so you have these other ones, also of the Orion energy, but they are somewhat like "missionaries" [as] they are traveling with the energy of Orion. You must remember that we are focusing energy into one and many of us are wanting to communicate with you, but only one can be voiced at a time, unless we collectively focus our energies into the channel [Krista].

How are you? We are here to speak with you about this Ascension process. Are you ready to ascend, friend? Well, we are many. Many, many angels with us here, today. Angels coming in to talk. Yes, we are Orion Council but angels [are] in this room, now. Do you understand what we mean by "angels in the room?" Angels are a special type of energy, you see, because they have to help humanity at this time. When you are connecting with God in your room and you are praying to God, you are asking angels to help you. You are asking angels to come to you and we are telling you that this is what is happening this very moment. The angels are in this room, watching this transmission of dialogue, friend. We are happy to discuss anything you would like to discuss.

Friend, you have sent us energy. We are feeling your energy signature. We recognize who you are. Interesting how this communication is not happening only through words. Much of the energies now are polarized, friend. Many are wanting Ascension; many do not want humanity to ascend. Many want the glamorous life. Many are wanting to use the light to veil the darkness. We do not discuss this because it is unnecessary for lightworkers to focus on the dark energy. Human beings are wanting to focus on the glamour of a star system. We say, you can do this focusing without becoming one with the energies you interact with. It is up to the lightworker if they want to incorporate this energy into their system.

[Many are feeling frustrated with physical reality.] It feels that way because you are in the duality. When a great Light Being has a limitation, sometimes it gets frustrated. That is understandable. How can you confine light in a box? It is something like this analogy: when you confine light in a box, it has to break out and shine. But we tell you, as we have told many before, that you wanted to have this experience.

The things that you are not liking are the ones helping you to focus on this Earth, you see. If you were to sing in a heavenly choir, perhaps you would float away. We do not want such a thing of your soul. You have a special task here, friend. You said you would become physical because you wanted to shine your light on the other ones. You said you would do this and so you are. Perhaps sometimes it feels as if you are not connected to Home. You look around and you see other ones asleep and you say, "Wake up, please. I'm tired of you sleeping." But we say, that bit by bit they are waking up. You do not see the big picture because of the duality. We want to remind you that you are with the angels, always. You will see the angels when you transition again. You will see us, as well. You are from Home and you are loved.

You came into this Earthly space because you asked to help the planet. You knew your Ascension depended on your help and so you came in with the intention to raise the vibration of the planet. The planet was suffering as it does, many times. The old energies were too heavy for Gaia. Many began to ask for God's interception. Many were living in the polarity of "not so good," for a long time, you see. This is why there were world wars. Yes, it is a replay of the past lessons, yes. However a new lesson constantly occurs because Earth, as you know, is a learning planet.

You must realize that you are multi-dimensional. When the veils are lifted in your physical life experience, you will see that all is transparent. This is why we call it *energy-reading*. Your energy is precious. Your energy is life-giving. Your energy holds much vibration that is needed to lift the planet's energies. At the moment, many on your planet are suffering because they are not wanting to release the past. Many are holding on as you say, "with dear life," to past events. The past was in place for certain reasons, and in order for the Earth to be a Mystery School, as some say, much had to be experienced for [the] soul's evolution. It seems as if the history of Earth was horrific. It seems as if past events should not have happened and we should have all lived in love, holding each other's hands, but the souls that came in needed to learn.

This is a new time and we guide many at this time to forgive history because it has happened, and now we are moving into a new beginning. All the signs are pointing to a benevolent future. The task now is for those on Earth to believe it is possible and to hold that vibration of it coming. Hold the vibration of the benevolent future and the benevolent "now" moment: this is the job of the lightworker. This is the job: to say that you have enjoyed your lifetime. Too many humans are focused on the past. Too many humans are focused on the hardships that have happened.

The energies of others will always exist. It is you who is the powerful Creator. We guide you to recall your Divine healing abilities and as you recall them, you will notice the other negative vibration wash away. Sometimes many of you human-friends absorb energy. We do not understand why a Creator would do such a thing but it is a mechanism, as if you were cleaning the planet. We see the purpose in this but we do not understand why humans would want to clean the planet in such a fashion. There are other ways to help the planet heal. You do not need to carry others' energies. You can simply transmute them, but that requires that you realize your own Divine healing power. It is a major thing to understand.

How can you serve? How can you bring in more light? Is that something that has been on your agenda? Do you feel that is part of your purpose? Good, because you are a good student, A+, you see. A++ because you are lightworker, yes? We are joking with you but we hope that you understand our humor. How can a human focus their light energy when they are distracted by the 3-D lifestyles of others? It is amazing how a lightworker can make it through this sort of life, when they are focusing on the love and so many are asleep. It is like they are on a separate television channel: they cannot comprehend what you are talking about when you talk about love. You are talking about something so foreign to them. They have never quite felt this love before and you have lived it your entire life. It is what your entire soul essence is about. You're vibrating on this new level of love that many humans are simply awakening to at this moment. It is part of your work and you have done so well. We hope you will continue to focus your love and shine it on others. It is quite important at this time, you see.

PART I: SESSIONS

DIALOGUES WITH THE ORION COUNCIL,
ARCHANGELS, AND OTHER BENEVOLENT
BEINGS OF LIGHT

Session 1

Orion Council: Orion Council, here. Why are you all waiting for us? We have been here for a long time.

Katherine: Well, we had to get ready for you.

Orion Council: We are always with you, wanting to talk with you; quite easy now. Well done. How are you?

Katherine: How are you?

Orion Council: Fine, thank you. We are fine. How are you?

Katherine: Krista just said something quite remarkable about her feeling of deep love for her family in a different way than before.

Orion Council: Yes. Ascension process is underway, you see. You are all feeling these acclimating energies. That is quite normal in the Ascension process. It is quite real and it is happening now.

Katherine: How beautiful is that!

Orion Council: Funny, funny that you would wonder if what you are feeling is real or not because it is quite real and we are telling you that you are quite right in your insights.

Katherine: Thank you. We have some questions for you.

Orion Council: We are ready for any question you have for us.

Katherine: Thank you. As you are a collective consciousness of eight —

Orion Council: Yes, we are eight.

Katherine: Do others channel you?

Orion Council: We have many channels for us, yes.

Katherine: All around the world?

Orion Council: Well, quite a few. We do not count because others are tapping in but they are not realizing who they are tapping into, you see.

Katherine: Is there a difference between you and the High Council of Orion?

Orion Council: We *are* the High Council of Orion. We are the High Council. We call it anything you want but High Council is quite correct. Good. Next question, please.

Katherine: What is your relationship to Krista?

Orion Council: We have been watching the Ascension process. Krista is creating a way of communication with us. She is opening her ability to awaken a mass of consciousness on the planet; awakening other people, her mission now.

(Editor's note: The Council is referring to Krista in her disembodied state which is observing the sessions.)

Katherine: Yes, she feels very strongly about that.

Orion Council: Wanting to help humanity is a main task for her but she wants to live a normal life, she says. So why does she feel so inclined to help? She wants to help herself, as well. It is not an easy task, you see.

Katherine: That's true. It's not an easy balancing act. How do you access our information?

Orion Council: When you are open, we have access to your thoughts.

Katherine: How is it that you have access to past events?

Orion Council: Well, we can look ahead and look behind, so we have many "eyes" in many places. We are not deliberately trying to look ahead or behind but we can upon request. We like to embark upon these missions of discovery because that is how your questions are answered. You want to look behind yourselves to learn the lessons of the past and so we can help you remember because we are able to look behind you in a sense, with our perception. We have come in with a capability to hold the light, so we can tap into light that extends through many dimensions. We can tap into the dimensions that are being accessed by the Higher Self and so it is through this Higher Self that we access your information. We are communicating with your Higher Selves at all times. When you are open, we have access and thus we are able to bring down the information that we are knowledgeable of. We are able to tap into your own experience, combining it with our own perceptions and give our insights about these subjects you are wanting to inquire about.

Katherine: How do we open to our Higher Selves?

Orion Council: We have to help you with that sometimes because many of you have hoped to tap in through meditation. It is not so easy because you are not so quite relaxed and you are not believing in the process of opening to your Higher Selves. It is always there but many are not believing and many are quite afraid of the Higher Self. It is ironic how you can be so fearful of something so beautiful and something that is who-you-truly-are. We tell you, the Higher Self is constantly overseeing the life tasks that you participate in. [It] is able to understand you and will not bother you on this Earth plane but when you are tapping into [it], the Higher Self is always tapping back and wanting to connect. It is simply a question of the frequency.

When you are focused upon physical reality you are bringing in the frequencies of the physical world and you are not focused on the Higher Self. The Higher Self is something so great. You have focus in many dimensions at the same time, in a sense, and we are telling you it is quite possible but it is not something you have practiced before. You are looking to the books and the teachers on how to escape your own minds and how to tap into this Higher, High Sense Perception. It is quite possible but when you are tapping into your High Sense Perception you have an avenue to the Higher Self. It is available at all times but it is very intense for some to tap into this energy.

Katherine: How are you able to assist us in tapping into our Higher Selves?

Orion Council: We want to discuss the Higher Self and tell you about its aspects, so this is why we enjoy answering your question and we would like to discuss the specifics of tapping into the Higher Self, you see. We have to tell you that there are many parts of the Higher Self that have not yet been expressed in the human existence on the planet. The Higher Self is wanting to express itself more and more but there are only so many ways you humans have to bring in this high energy. We can tell you that when you are focusing upon the light within yourselves, that is bringing in the Higher Self to your physical reality, and you are helping to elevate the energies on the planet. We say that you must remember to focus the light within because that is how you will begin to bring in the Higher Self. It is a question of focus, first and foremost.

Katherine: When you say, "focusing the light within" do you mean the light within one's own consciousness?

Orion Council: Yes, correct. You must remember to focus the light within because that is how you will begin to bring in the Higher Self. You asked this question before about focusing the light and so we continue this question-and-answer.

Katherine: I ask that again because I realized that you must be referring to light within consciousness and not a physical form of light within the body.

Orion Council: You are constantly focusing on the specifics of how the light is brought in. It is, of course, through the consciousness as well. Your awakened Self is what is aware of the entire process but you are bringing in the light. You are feeling the light through the pores of your skin and your entire awareness. So if that is consciousness to you, then yes, you are correct. Consciousness is many things. It is used as the reference to the mind but the mind is only lone way to focus the light. You have many feelers for bringing in the light.

Katherine: Could you go back to the many parts or aspects of the Higher Self that are not yet being expressed in human experience?

Orion Council: The Higher Self has many aspects and wishes to incorporate them into the physical world but it is not quite possible because the Earth Plane does not support these elevated energies. So many unseen things would begin to be seen, it would not be comfortable to the masses. Can you remember the last time you saw a unicorn? You would not feel comfortable because your mind is not yet equipped to handle such a thing. It would be quite detrimental to many to see [such] things starting to appear. The Higher Self, of course, is a very magical device. It has many capabilities and so if you were to bring in these capabilities, you could, as a human race, create much destruction upon the planet.

Katherine: Okay, that's one; perhaps another aspect?

Orion Council: Higher Self also wants to speak of God and so it would be a constant discussion of God and a search for God.

(Editor's note: Please use whatever term that resonates with you: God, The Creator, Source, All-That-Is, The Divine, Source Energy, Great Spirit, The Infinite Invisible, Prime Mover, Ntr, etc.)

We would like to tell you that God is always with us and God wants us to have our experiences but the Higher Self is constantly in communication with God and would constantly want to bring in more God-like aspects to the physical world. Can you believe that there is more light that exists and that it is constantly evolving? There are many new realities for you all to experience. Even at this very moment the Higher Self is experiencing other realities and so those other realities could be incorporated your natural environment as well, but that would change many things, you see. There would be many processes changing with one simple idea. This is why we must say to you that to filter the Higher Self is wisest at this moment. What are you all wanting to experience? When you have enough wanting to experience something new, that is when it begins to happen. The mass consciousness is able to handle this new experience coming in, you see, because enough souls are wanting the same thing. That is the beauty of the Collective Consciousness and the togetherness of humanity on the planet because enough people wanting change could change the entire planet and [its] makeup but that would not be wise because it is a learning place for many souls. So you do not want to completely change this learning place. It is not fair to the other ones. You would want the order in the world because it is serving many at this time, you see. If you were wanting to dance with the unicorns, perhaps you could do this in a world that is of unicorns. You can manifest what you want on this Earth but you would not want to disrupt the entire order of the planet. You would want the highest good to happen and the Higher Self is always wanting the highest good because it is constantly in communication with God, you see.

God is wanting the best for all. Higher Self is wanting you to know who you are and wanting you to know what you are doing upon the planet. Higher Self is asking for your awareness of these topics that you are quite interested in at this moment. Higher Self wants you to persist in your search for God and reality and so on, and so on, and so on. It always continues. Higher Self is made up of many parts and many focuses, many focused attention points, you see. So, what are you wanting to know about Higher Self? Are you wanting to know where it is focusing? It is focusing in many interesting realities but is that what you are looking for?

Katherine: No, I have a general understanding of the multi-dimensional aspects of the Higher Self.

Orion Council: It is disruptive to your Earthly experience because you are wanting certain things but you are not wanting others. So, you must discern what it is you are wanting.

Katherine: Do we each have, in a sense, a separate Higher Self?

Orion Council: What a good question. The Higher Self is collective energies, so you are sharing Higher Selves with other people, as well. It is not that there is one Higher Self for all of humanity. There are many Higher Selves but you can tap into the same Higher Self with another energy because All Is One. They are not numeric in the same sense that we say we are eight but we cannot say there are eight Higher Selves. It is a different dynamic on the different planes of existence. On one plane you will have the number two. On another plane you would have the infinite possibilities of two, you see. Quite interesting you would ask this question because we know you are wanting to learn more about the makeup of the Spirit World and wanting to write it in human terms. It is possible and we could tell you but that would be a distortion in a sense, to give you so many numbers and so many figures. Many have done this. Many are interested in the geometries and those are quite valid. They are not disruptive to the makeup of the universe because they are focused on the tiniest particles that are making up this physical world. When you are asking how the Spirit World is made up, it is not the same sort of crystalline structure that you are made up of. It is something so beautiful — it is difficult to describe in human terms. In the Spirit World there are many, many evolutionary theories that are constantly, constantly considered and constantly woven into realities, so to speak. So when you are wanting to know the beauty of it all, we say it is constantly evolving and it is like a cell that is constantly multiplying. So how can you give a number to something that is constantly evolving?

Katherine: It is not possible, is it?

Orion Council: Quite right. Good question, Katherine. We are noticing your potential to understand and we are quite aware that you are the one who is ready to ask many, many new questions that will help others on their quest to ascend to these higher planes of existence. Your task is to help the other ones who are not quite understanding. And you are quite right to ask these questions. We are wanting to help you, however, we must say that you must take one step at a time.

Session 2

Katherine: For today's session, I'd like to begin by saying a prayer: Kodoish, Kodoish, Kodoish, Adonai Tsebayoth. [Holy, Holy, Holy, is the Lord God of Hosts]

Orion Council: Okay. Yes. Good. Hello.

Katherine: Hello, welcome.

Orion Council: Good. Wonderful. Can you train her to pray more?

Katherine: I will suggest it.

Orion Council: We are glad you are praying. Can you help to train her? We are here to discuss your Ascension. How many of us do you think there are today? We are listening to your prayer energy.

Katherine (Joking): I will take a wild guess and say eight.

Orion Council: You are correct. We are eight, Katherine, eight.

Katherine: Welcome.

Orion Council: We are glad to be here today.

Katherine: You are most welcome. We are glad you are here with us today. You said you wanted to discuss Ascension?

Orion Council: Yes. You are quite right that humans understand their multi-dimensional realities more and more than before. Your friend at the fair today, what is she doing? How is she going about her business? *(Ed. note: Katherine attended a New Age exhibition and conversed with one of the vendors.)* Well, can you imagine what it is like when a person does not know who they are? Many people are tapping into their potentials but still do not realize who they are.

Katherine: And isn't that key?

Orion Council: Yes. You must come with that understanding to all endeavors in your life, you see. That is the goal now. Many are looking outside for outer reflections. That is correct but you have to carry around the knowing that you are hundreds of millions of countries and countries are galaxies. Galaxies are where you are all from, you see. You are all from different galaxies. Do you understand?

Katherine: Yes.

Orion Council: Okay. First of all, your soul is o-o-old. Your soul is so fine; it is of light fibers. Your soul is made up of millions of light fibers. Okay, what are you wanting to ask us today? You are old soul.

Katherine: Well, let me ask you about that.

Orion Council: Yes, you are o-o-old soul.

Katherine: Isn't that true of everybody or is there a mixture of old and new souls?

Orion Council: Old souls here now in this time; you know that. Many are old souls. Old souls incarnating now because Ascension process already has begun. You need older ones to show the way. Old souls have the old feelings, they don't move so quickly like the younger souls:

they are wanting to watch them play, you see. Watching TV but not quite, they are wanting to witness Ascension as well – they want to see how it unfolds. They want to watch from the sidelines but they have a multi-dimensional task to accomplish at this time.

Katherine: The old ones, you mean?

Orion Council: Yes. Many dimensions are active because Ascension has begun and by tapping into these elements of existence, we have to say that it is not easy to remember where you came from because these elements are part of your make up. They just are not where you came from. They are active now because you have now accessed the new grids that are constructed in the ethers. These levels of existence are within your own soul makeup and they are multi-dimensional layers of existence.

Katherine: Very fascinating.

Orion Council: Okay, you have to remember that we have to tell you about Ascension because that is why we have come in to talk with you. We want to discuss Ascension because it is so important at this time.

Katherine: Can you give us a definition of Ascension?

Orion Council: Yes. Good question; it's anticipated. What is that Ascension? Well, human beings are forgetting who they are, so we are here to tell you that you are from many galaxies and you are all quite content with this Earth [and] we want you to continue to feel content with this Earth. When you are feeling content —

Krista (Interjecting): Mom, they are talking about Gaia. It's a stream of information — lessons.

Orion Council: We are talking about Gaia, yes. We are talking about this process of Ascension because many are not remembering who they are and it is time. Many are remembering, too. Okay now, so where are we standing, you ask? How many remember and how many do not remember? What do we do with those who don't? Throw them to the lions, yes? Okay, joking. Of course, you know we are joking because it is our humor. Okay, throw them to the lions but not yet, give a chance first. Okay?

Katherine: Okay. Shine a little light on them first.

Orion Council: Yes. Other ones need assistance; need assistance badly right now. It's a wonderful time to assist others. You have to come to terms with who you are first, though. You have to remember that you are important at this time. You need to focus the light within yourself first, okay? Katherine, that is for you. Katherine, you need to focus more light on yourself; shine the light on yourself. Katherine you must do this. It is our, well – kind of demand, not exactly.

Katherine: I understand. Thank you.

Orion Council: You are favorite. You are so beautiful, Katherine. Okay, many of us want to talk but I think you are beautiful. Goodbye.

Katherine: Goodbye. Oh, wait!

Orion Council: Okay. Yes?

Katherine: What...how can I call you?

Orion Council: We are eight. Eight of us.

Katherine: I remember your energy.

Orion Council: You remember. Good.

Katherine: It is very distinct.

Orion Council: You do remember; you can tell the difference.

Katherine: Yes. I think Krista calls you "mother."

(Ed. note: The different intelligences of the Orion Council have labeled themselves as "scientist", "mother" and "training officer." They take turns speaking, depending upon the questions asked of them.)

Orion Council (Humorously): Oh, am I a mother? Maybe I am.

Katherine: Maybe, maybe not.

Orion Council: Maybe you will find out one day. Do I have kids?

(Laughter)

Orion Council: Okay, other people want to speak too. Not so much "people" but you know what we mean.

Katherine: Yes, I do, thank you.

Orion Council: *Buon giorno!*

Katherine: *Buon giorno, come stai?*

Orion Council: Eh! Okay. Our turn, now. All right. Okay. Many of us want to talk now. We are having good time tonight; it's a party. Yes, all right, you have to have fun with this, too. It's not a serious game. Ha, ha, ha – Serious. It is not "Sirius." You understand our joke? It is not a "Sirius" game. You get it, Sirius? It is a place. Get the place? We are having a joke but it is not [an] understandable one. Okay, what would you like to discuss with us today?

Katherine: The "Big A."

Orion Council: We have to tell you about Ascension because it is time for humans to remember who they are.

Katherine: Is that basically what Ascension is all about?

Orion Council: Well, hold on...My, my, my, it is nice to talk again. Many of us wanting to say hello to you.

Katherine: Hello!

Orion Council: Hello! Okay, you are getting to know us now because you have the intention to write a book. So many of us want to talk you see. We have different energies when we come through. We all want our turn, you see, so please have patience with us.

Katherine: Of course, of course.

Orion Council: Okay. Hello. My, my, here we are. You are sensing our energies now, you are sensing, yes? Can you tell the difference between our energies?

Katherine: Yes.

Orion Council: Okay, so many of us here, wanting to assist

you in the Ascension process. We are all glad to be able to talk with you; it is amazing to be able to talk to you like this.

Katherine: Quite amazing.

Orion Council (Whispering): My, my, it is amazing. We are so glad to talk with you; you cannot understand how amazing it is. We are learning to talk with you through the channel [Krista].

Katherine (Also whispering): Yes, quite astounding isn't it?

Orion Council (Mock indignation): You are imitating us! We are glad to have this opportunity because you have asked for us to come in and we are saying, we come when you ask us. We are enjoying this communication immensely at this moment. The intensity is strong. You are feeling this intensity; that is why we whisper. It's beautiful. It's so beautiful on this side you cannot imagine it. It is so beautiful, Katherine.

Katherine: On which side?

Orion Council: This side of the veil. It is beautiful to see you like this. We are seeing you with the channel; we are seeing you now —

Katherine: I need you to please speak a little louder so that we get this on the recording.

Orion Council: Yes, okay, good job to ask us that. We will lift our voices.

Katherine: Thank you. What were you saying?

Orion Council: It is so beautiful to see you from this per-spective; in the channel. About time. It's good to have a cold because the channel says it helps [her] to step aside.

[You] do not enjoy the body so much so you want to step out of it [when ill]. It is like [being] ready to pass over because you are ill. It is like that. So, good time to channel when you are not feeling so well. Perfect time.

Katherine: That's a different perspective.

Orion Council: Yes it is. There is always use for everyone.

Katherine: So, about Ascension?

Orion Council: Okay. Ascension is what is going on now.

Katherine: Everything is ascending? Gaia herself?

Orion Council: Everyone, yes.

Katherine: Our whole solar system? Our current awareness of it, anyway. Is that correct? The sun, the other planets?

Orion Council: [The] sun is focused on the planetary shifts. Sun is wanting us all to remember who we are, as well, but sun is doing its own thing too, you see. Sun is also a life-force energy, a form of life as well, and in the sun there are other beings too, you see. They are the solar ones. You can have names for them but the solar ones, generally speaking, are here to unite humanity in this moving energy. They are the ones who like the fire. They are setting things aflame to get people moving across borders and so on. They want people to travel more, so they start fires sometimes. They want them to leave the place, like Russian fire. *(Ed. note: there were hundreds of forest fires in Russia in 2010, as a result of unusually high temperatures.)* Krista has trouble saying it. Inside of the Earth is a realm of Beings of Light, too. They are wanting

Ascension, too. They are happy to ascend with humanity because now the energies are perfect to ascend. They will celebrate the Ascension with us. All of us are celebrating but it is the humans who must remember who they are. You are the special ones, in a sense. The universe is watching you all now. Do you feel that you are being watched?

Katherine (Humorously): By a million-billion eyes!

Orion Council: Are you sure? You are correct! So, what can we do for you now?

Katherine: How do we —

Orion Council: Hold the light?

Katherine: Yes, hold the light.

Orion Council: You hold the light with a match. Ha, ha! You hold the light with your intention and your intention must be for the highest good to happen at all times. Okay, okay, let us slow down, it is not so easy. When your intention is pure, as she, the channel has been learning – she says, "Commentary, add onto book." She says that [it] needs to have the highest, pure intention. [She] is correct but sometimes people dismiss themselves. So when it does not feel right, they sometimes think they are giving unto others but still [are] forgetting [their] own needs. Good. So now what are "own needs?" Eating of food, shelter? You have other needs as well: holding your own hand when you are afraid. You have to hold your own hand at all times because you are your own best friend. It is not a simple saying; it is profound. A question?

Katherine: When you were expanding on holding the light,

29

holding one's own hand, in addition to assisting others, "healer heal thyself" —

Orion Council: Oh. . .pardon. . . Please. . . pardon.. . Problems listening. Krista did not listen.

Katherine: Shall I repeat? The question was about holding the light.

Orion Council: "Healer heal thyself," you said. Good job, Katherine.

Katherine: I guess my question is my concern —

Orion Council: You have so many concerns: out the window, goodness! We are joking.

Katherine: I wish that it were that easy to just chuck them out the window.

Orion Council: How to maintain this Earthly experience when you want to focus on the light?

Katherine: Yes, but actually the other way around: how to focus the light when we are embroiled in this human experience?

Orion Council (Humorously): Embroiled? Like chickens in a coop!

Katherine: Like chickens on a spit, being roasted.

Orion Council: We are saying that when you are focusing on negativities, that is your experience. You know this but it is not easy. It seems that human beings are wondering when the good things will happen to them. If we say, "tomorrow," will it happen tomorrow? Always skeptical, humans are: conditioned to think that there is no good and you must have rainbows ten times a day for anything good to happen to you. You all know that when good happens, it is because you made it happen. So think of making good things in your life, think of how your life has been formed. Who created your life? Your parents did not create your life. After you left home, [they] did not create your life. Who created your life? Your partner? Your sister? Your brother?

Katherine: One's self. Yourself. Myself.

Orion Council: Correct. So, when you are knowing that you have created all of it, you have come to where you are now – and have you created that as well?

Katherine: Yes.

Orion Council: Correct. So who's going to create the future? You, your friend, us?

Katherine: Me.

Orion Council: You; that is correct. So when you know this, you must remember and you must remember and so on, and so on, and so on. Put a paper on your Facebook. Put a paper on your face. Can you understand?

Katherine: I understand exactly. Wear it on your nose, if necessary [to remember].

Orion Council: We are glad you understand our comment; it is not a normal comment. My, it is good to speak with you. We are all here now to listen and to help. Many of us, wanting to help right now. Many of us, wanting to communicate.

Katherine: You are doing it one at a time, it seems.

Orion Council: You understand the process; good.

(Break in session)

Orion Council: We are glad that you had a break because it is time for us to discuss Ascension. We are glad that you are asking us these questions because you are remembering who you are. So, when you ask you get closer to your own soul, in a way. When you are focusing the light within yourself, you are an example — walking through the Earth — of someone who holds their light, you see: a light-bearer, a light beacon, a lightworker holding the light, knowing you are light, when others do not; knowing that they are light, when they do not.

Katherine: Holding the light is —

Orion Council: .You are holding the light now; you are feeling that light.

Katherine: Yes, I am.

Orion Council: You are focusing on that light, now.

Katherine: And as you mentioned yesterday, using the mantras and affirmations —

Orion Council: Please, say them again.

Katherine: Ehyeh Asher Ehyeh. [I Am That I Am]

Orion Council: .Wow. All right God is listening when you say that.

Katherine: Ehyeh Asher Ehyeh . . . Nuk pu Nuk.

Orion Council: You are so wonderful.

Katherine: When we say that, we are focusing the light? Is that correct?

Orion Council: Correct.

Katherine: I feel as if I could say that all day, sometimes.

Orion Council: That's correct because that is where you are from, you see.

Katherine: Yes. Source. Why do you use the word God as opposed to Source or Spirit?

Orion Council: It's a common one many will know.

Katherine: Okay. In terms of Ascension, the babies that are coming in now, and will be coming in such as Krista's and Kier's children someday —

Orion Council: They are wide awake.

Katherine: Old souls?

Orion Council: Yes, of course.

Katherine: And they have already selected their mother, Krista?

Orion Council: Well, one has his eye on her. Yes, he's been watching her a long time. Wants to be with mommy. It's about time but not quite yet. She's not ready yet. Must hold the light within, first. She has to get up and focus the light within herself. She must remember who she is and why she came here. "This time is going to be different," she said. She said she would help her friends on the planet

Earth and now she's helping them. She's helping those who need to hear her words.

Katherine: Are you referring to her internet contacts?

Orion Council: [It is] one avenue of communication. She's got many avenues of communication available.

Katherine: What others?

Orion Council: Partially concerning the process of awakening. This time she's got to focus light within and use her head. She does not use her head, she's using her emotions. She must use her head, come on. She must use her head to manage these ideas. All over the place sometimes; must focus sometimes.

Katherine: Easily distracted, sometimes?

Orion Council: Perfect response, yes.

Katherine: I will help her with that.

Orion Council: Good, thank you. My turn. Hello.

Katherine: Hello. Welcome.

Orion Council: Thank you. Good evening. Time for us to applaud you because you have the courage to speak up about certain topics. You have many lifetimes of being withheld. You've not been able to discuss your topics of interest because you were shunned by others. Now you have the chance to say what you want to say. You've got to remember that you came in with a talent —"gift of gab." You say things correctly. People understand where you are coming from. You communicate in many ways not just your words, your attitude – and your focused energy is so attractive to others.

Katherine: Excuse me for interrupting but are you speaking of Krista and I?

Orion Council: You, Katherine. Must focus but you have got that gift of focusing. Krista is so scattered; must focus.

Katherine: I will help her.

Orion Council: Good, but you have got that skill. Must remember your own purpose is to "face the music."

Katherine: What does that mean?

Orion Council: It's not all so peachy and keen on this Earth. Many have to focus their light intentionally. We are here to discuss more of this purpose. You've got to remember your purpose is to help those who do not remember who they are. It's a lot [to] ask of a person, it's a lot [to] ask of you. When the world was perfect — ha, ha, ha, — when the world was perfect, it was magnificent for all. Everyone shared and everyone helped one another. Everyone remembered who they were. They knew that they were of God and so they loved themselves and they loved one another. It was all in cooperation, and communication was simple; not so distorted as it is now. [For example] cannot understand what people want and why they say things. Are they jaded? Are they with some kind of preoccupation with whatever the topic is or are they simply talking for the sake of it?

Katherine: When the world was perfect, was that a different dimension?

Orion Council: Well that was when the Murians were

here.

Katherine: The Lemurians?

Orion Council: Murians. Murians.

Katherine: Murians from Mu? *(Ed. note: Pronounced "mew")*

Orion Council: You are right on target. Mu was a time when the human was inside the Earth and was Ascending but was in the Earth, you see. They were inside the Earth, too.

Katherine: Why do you say, "too?"

Orion Council: They were inside the Earth and had to focus light on top of the Earth to heal the outer layer of the Earth.

Katherine: Why did it need healing if everything was perfect?

Orion Council: It was needing a fix; it had a collision.

Katherine: With what?

Orion Council: Had a collision happen with another Earth. Mu was colliding with another Earth. Earth was colliding with Mu; Mu was colliding with Earth. My, how is it you are not getting it? Mu was colliding with Earth.

Katherine: You're making it sound as if they are two separate things.

Orion Council: It was one thing but they collided. Inside of the Earth was Mu and it collided with the Earth. My, it is not an easy concept; apparently it is not making any sense.

Katherine: Well, you did say that we are talking about the surface and we are talking about within, so that helps.

Orion Council: So it collides with the surface; is that not possible? The inner aspect collided with the surface. They became one, yet were somehow separate. In time they became one. Much like what is happening now except that you are colliding with the Earth in a new way.

Katherine: Are you talking about continental drift, for example?

Orion Council: No! We are talking about the Ascension. It is like when two humans meet, then they mate and become one energy; much like Murians. Murians.

Katherine: All right.

Orion Council (Emphatically): Much to learn. Must remember to heal the Earth and you become one with the Earth again.

Katherine: The Murians, may I ask you a question about them?

Orion Council: You may. Much to learn.

Katherine: Were these —

Orion Council: — Etheric beings, yes. Question is well formed. We know your questions sooner than you think.

Katherine: Sooner than *I* think of them, it seems! I appreciate your patience.

Orion Council: We are enjoying your cooperation. Mu was a time when the humans were not so dense: they had to feel with their hearts and hear with their ears but they had no hair. They were somewhat like the apes but not quite; they were more human. They had their aspects like a dried up prune. They had those kinds of skins.

Katherine: Wrinkled?

Orion Council: Yes, wrinkled; they were wrinkly and had their own way of talking about themselves, as well. It was positive and they enjoyed the Ascension process because they knew they were becoming something new. They were changing and they knew they were changing. So it was enjoyed because they loved what they were and they loved who they were becoming.

Katherine: Is that very different from now?

Orion Council: Yes, many are afraid they will explode into smithereens but it is not happening; they will not explode. These people now are thinking they need some special equipment or they are needing some sort of savior, but they are the ones who are saving themselves.

Katherine: Is it simply a question of belief? If you believe that some savior, or if you believe some crystal, will save you, or if you believe that you will save yourself — will it not be so, according to your belief?

Orion Council: Yes, good question. That is quite right. It is all a question of matters of consciousness and where you stand in your consciousness. If you are standing somewhere far from reality — you know what we mean — then you are not quite aware that your beliefs form the reality around you, so you will think that you are separate when you are a part of All-That-Is. It is a question of believing: if you believe that you are separate, you will behave in that manner. If you believe you are focusing light, you will focus light. If you believe you deserve to have money, you will have money. If you love yourself, you will show the world how much love there is for everyone because you will be the one shining the light for all to see and it is authentic so others will enjoy that light.

Katherine: Thank you, that was quite beautiful.

Orion Council: Much appreciated. We enjoy this discussion. Pardon us, we have many here wanting to discuss these things – all matters human. Must remember to heal yourself. Good question. We were discussing the Ascension of the planet and we offered you help with your light focusing. We want to discuss this because it is material for your work. Good, now you know what we are doing. Many of us wanting to talk with you today. What are you wanting to ask us today?

Katherine: The planet has ascended many times, yes?

Orion Council: Yes, it has before and it will again. My, these times are what eventually will happen yet again, you see. It will repeat another time and another time. It is a never ending learning process. It is a place where selves go to learn how to grow and ascend. There are many opportunities available on this Earth, you see. There are many options for your learning. This will happen yet again — "Just like the Atlantis story," says the Keeper [Krista]. "It was three trials," she says, [of] Atlantis not working. Anyway, this Ascension will happen again. This is a learning place, a learning planet.

Katherine: Is this particular time of Ascension different in that we don't have to be destroyed in order to ascend?

Orion Council: Well, there was never a destruction. There was a transition only.

Katherine: Even Atlantis?

Orion Council: Yes, a transition period. A story others want you to remember because it is a teaching story.

Katherine: Are you saying there was no fall?

Orion Council: No, we are saying it is a wonderful story that happened in life but it is not happening again, it is simply a question of this repetitive process of growing and learning. Many at this time are wanting to know what happened with Atlantis because that sounds so beautiful. Indeed these times are changing and people are wondering if it will be just like Atlantis but it can be how you want it to be. These Creators do not realize that they are the ones who make the next move. If you want it to be like Atlantis again, it will be. It is up to the Creators on the Earth. That is why many of you come back, you see. We say things as if they repeat themselves automatically but they are simply...well, Ascension happens in intervals. Ascension happens in intervals. In the future you will have another Ascension but it will be a learning process again. It is one pattern happening over and over again on this Earth.

Katherine: Why is it that we do not remember? Did we agree to put on the veil of forgetfulness?

Orion Council: Well asked. Yes, you have asked a good question. Well said. This is the time when you want to learn that humans need to help one another; this is the time for learning this kind of lesson. This kind of lesson is important and in Atlantis many were helping but many were [also] not helping each other. So, destruction occurred because these helpers so badly wanted to help, but the other ones wanted to use this against them. The other ones were saying, "No, you cannot help others, you must only help yourself; forget about the other ones." It sounds ironic but now it is almost the other way around: you must help yourselves but at the same time help others. It is like a balancing act. Both sides must be helped.

Katherine: And that's a lesson this time around?

Orion Council: This time you all need to remember who you are. This time you all need to focus the light within yourselves and have a balance within all areas of life.

Katherine: Was there a reason for coming here without remembering that?

Orion Council: Yes, the reason was to help you with this focusing energy, you see. If your focused energy is everywhere, like Krista, how will you create a book? We are joking, but when you are focusing on Atlantis and the other places you want to visit in your dream space, how can you focus on this "now" reality? You would forget easily what your task was. You need this focus so you needed to forget; you needed to focus on [the] simple, three dimension. It's a simple place. So, this is why you wanted to forget. It is so simple. Almost simple, but not quite simple. To the human it is not simple at all, it is most complex.

Katherine: And painful.

Orion Council: That is correct.

Katherine: Is 3D no longer?

Orion Council: It is existing at the same time. There are ones who want to forget about it already, we can tell, but it is still existing for many.

Katherine: Where are we right now?

Orion Council: Fourth dimension here.

Katherine: Ehyeh Asher Ehyeh. I Am That I am.

Orion Council: You Are That You Are. My, it is late. You must all fall asleep. We are glad you are asking us these questions because you are needing confirmation. We understand that now.

Katherine: Yes, we do. That's all right with you?

Orion Council: Quite all right.

Katherine: I do have a couple more questions, if that's okay.

Orion Council: Tiring, but a good time to ask.

Katherine: What is this spinning sensation that we've both been experiencing?

Orion Council: Those are those chakras, active. Which one is overactive now?

Katherine: The crown?

Orion Council: Yes, good job! Your head and your crown, so open now. Can you see and feel the buzz? You have to ground yourself afterwards. Health is the sense of well-being. You will feel that, when you have those in balance. You will have to balance chakras to become healthy again. Balance your chakras, work with your chakras, and you will gain your sense of well-being back.

Katherine: What do we have to do to balance them?

Orion Council: You must focus the light within each, one at a time. See light pouring into them: all of them being cleaned; all of them having their own separate task; all of them knowing what to do, all of them different sizes and shapes and colors, similar but different, all having their own things to do for your body. All of them knowing they are pure light energy: your beautiful chakra centers of light! Know that they are your helpers in the Ascension process. Know that you are made of Liquid Light. Know that your healing hands are helping others to heal. Remember that healing can happen in other dimensions. You can ask other Beings of Light in other realms to send you healing energy for certain parts of the body that need light energy there. Remember protection and to ask the angels for protection and then you will be fine. You are fine. You are part of this Ascension because you decided you wanted to help other people, and you also wanted other people to recognize your Spirit. So when you meet similar souls, remember to thank them and tell them how happy you are to be in their presence. Old souls here now, many of them here. You will meet many more. You must simply focus the light within them and see that which what you want to see.

Katherine: I look forward to the meeting.

Orion Council: You will meet many other like-minded

ones. You still have time here, Katherine. You still have time.

Katherine: On this planet? You mean, in this human experience?

Orion Council: Yes. You are a wonderful lightworker, Katherine. Loving you so much; God is loving you so much. We are finished. We will like to talk with you again tomorrow or another day.

Katherine: Thank you very much for coming.

Orion Council: My pleasure.

Katherine: All of you.

Orion Council: All of us. Bye.

Katherine: Good bye.

Session 3

Krista: Today, I feel drunk with happiness and I'm looking around Mom's room appreciating everything. It's this euphoria sweeping through me and I'm just smiling. I tend to laugh before the channeling happens; I know that means that they are connecting. The Council abruptly came through today, to tell us to focus on our health. Sometimes my entire body seems to get extremely tired before they come in and I almost shut down; I think I'm learning control. Now, they are here, so I'm laughing; it's a good connection. My body feels so good! I feel like I just had a massage. I don't want to go. I feel so good, I don't want to go right now.

Katherine: Let's say our prayer. Ready? Kodoish, Kodoish, Kodoish —

Krista: No, that feels too good; I can't go there yet!

Katherine: — Adonai Tsebayoth.

Krista (Laughing): Mom, no, no, that's too intense, that draws them right in.

Katherine: — Kodoish, Kodoish, Kodoish —

Krista: I don't want to go yet; I don't want to channel; I want to stay here feeling good! It feels like they're tickling me. I don't want to go. Don't say it. I don't want them to come in yet.

Orion Council: We are here, hello.

Katherine: Hello, welcome.

Orion Council: It's been a good time tonight. She is acclimating the energies, yes? Acclimating energies, feeling so wonderful, yes? Well, we have to tell you about the Ascension happening now, okay? It's stronger than before. Ascension was not as strong as it is now. Many are saying that it has been so difficult but we are saying it is easy to ascend, now. You are awake; it is easy to ascend. It's so simple; you focus on the light and then light happens. It's so good, isn't it? That's how it should be. When you are loving your family, that is 5th dimension, of course. It is amazing how you all connect with each other, now. You are all doing so well, you are all healing old hurts, old things that no longer serve you, old things that have passed. Old things have gone now, okay? It's old, goodbye, it's old, goodbye, it's old, goodbye. We are saying goodbye because it exists —of course [there is] no time, but the past is not important. It is there but it helped you come to where you are now. Okay? It was a good thing but now you have to move on from old things.

You know that but we will state this to assist you with the Ascension process. Many are focusing on themselves now, which is a good thing. Before, it was always about focusing on others but now you are focusing on yourselves – so important. We have to tell you about Ascension because it is happening now, okay? You are all feeling these new energies coming in and they are of the light, they are good. They are infinite possibilities occurring in your waking states. You are realizing that you have infinite potential and you all will ascend together. It is a quite wonderful feeling of Ascension. My, how many of you are ascending. So many want to know how many are ascending. We say all are ascending but some are not remembering to focus the light within themselves, so they are caught between these energies and they are feeling discord because they are not focused on the light within themselves. So, when they are not doing so, they are angry and frustrated.

It is time to think of good thoughts, now. It's time to be happy now, you see. It's time to enjoy life, now. Have had hard times. Many on Earth have had hardships, so now is the time for good [to] come in. More good is coming in; you can't believe how good comes in, but it will begin to speed up. It will begin to speed up.

Katherine: May I ask you a question? Even though you are saying good is "coming in," would I be correct in saying that it is not so much "coming in" as it always has been there, always will be there, and that we are awakening to it? Allowing it in?

Orion Council: You are Wise One; wise woman you are. You understand the whole game, you do. Well, you are remembering that when you are focused on the light, it is something always existing, but before it was not focused upon so much. This time, many humans are wanting to feel good. So, [whereas] this energy has been around, it's time to bring more into this Earthly experience. You are correct that it will always exist because energy is always good energy.

(Another energy enters): Going to describe to you centuries-old things, centuries-old kinds of practices. Golden Age of Atlantis was good. Yes, a good time but can we say it was not going so well at end of Atlantis. Going, going, g-g, golden. Golden Age was not so well arranged. It was not well arranged, yes?

Katherine: Why are we talking about the Golden Age of Atlantis now?

(Slow speech): It was a good time. Well, you've got to focus on the light, so when you talk about this . . . Communication . . . hold on. It's not so easy for us now. We have come in to speak with you.

Katherine: Who are you?

(Extremely slow speech): Yes. . . going. . . to. . .talk. . . Going. . . Hard. . . Golden Age was. . . Hold on. . . It's us. . Gorgeous. . . gorgeous time. . . have to help her.

Katherine: Who's speaking now, please?

(Softly): Angels.

Katherine: Which angels?

(Gently): Angels. . .of. . .hard. . . to. . say. . Hard. . to. . say. Angel. . .Golden. . .Angel.

Katherine: All right.

Angel: Hello.

Katherine: Hello.

Angel: It's Golden Angel.

Katherine: What do you want to share with us today?

Angel: Angel of White Light. . . Help her.

Katherine: Are you all right, Krista?

Angel: Healing herself now.

Katherine: Krista is healing herself?

Angel: Yes. Healing herself. Angels are helping healing her. Angel of Golden Light, here.

Katherine: May I ask you a question?

Angel: Well, yes.

Katherine: What does she need to healed of?

Angel: Appreciation . . .Appreciation.

Katherine: She needs to appreciate herself?

Angel: Yes!

Katherine: And that's what you're helping her with?

Angel: My, yes.

Katherine: Well, thank you for that.

Angel: Angel of Golden Light, here. Yes, I want to help her. I have to help her. So many are needing a lot of wonderful ways to live. We are angels trying "crazy hard" to help amuse you. Angels are only of the light. Angels of the Light, here. Nice to talk with you. My, it's beautiful to see you. My, it's beautiful to see you; you have golden energy. You have got friends here of light. Angels helping you, too.

Katherine: Thank you very much.

Angel: Nice to talk with you. Nice to talk about the light. My goodness, we are all here. Nice to talk with you. Angels are beautiful and want your help with the Earth. We are asking you to help Gaia, too. It is time for Gaia to love herself more. Gaia needs to love herself; it's time to help

Gaia heal the past, too . . .You all have felt this energy; helping is a nice thing.

Katherine: How can we help Gaia?

Angel: You have to tell Gaia you love her. Can you tell her? Helping Gaia is doing service; it's a good service. We have to tell you about healing your own hearts, too. Nice to talk with you. Remember the angels are here helping you, too. It's time to go. My, you are so beautiful. We have to tell you that it's good to talk and good to welcome us in at times. You have to welcome in angels. Angels are going to creating help for you; wanting to help you. Angels wanting to help Katherine, too. Nice to see you.

We are coming to say our thanks to you and helping you is our job. It's our turn to help you, too. It's awakening process. It's time to create with angels, too. No waiting anymore. Nice to see you, beautiful Being of Light. You've got something magical by your side. You've got many here with you, I am one: Angel of Golden Light. I am your friend. I am here. Have you forgotten me? I was your Angel of course. My, you are gorgeous. Yes. Angel of Golden Energies. I'm one. I have help, too. It's my way of saying, "love you. I love you." Angels are helping you, too.

Katherine: Thank you. Do you hear when we ask of you?

Angel: Of course, always here.

Katherine: Thank you very much.

Angel: Why don't you ask for our help? It's time to talk with us. Got to help you; our job. You [also] have to help yourself; it's your game. Your game, yes. You have to help yourself. Tuning to energies is an amazing way to heal. Yes, try to focus on your goals in life. How do you want to achieve them? Why do you want them? Why do you achieve these things? How are you feeling at the time when you have to become one with angels? Angels are trying quickly to attune... creating your happiness, we are trying to help you with happiness. You have a way of saying you don't feel good but you can with angelic help, feeling good, helping you to feel good. You have asked for us and we have come; it is time for us to talk with you. You have to hold back when there is trouble. You have to hold back.

Katherine: What do you mean?

Angel: You have to hold back your own energy. You have to hold it back. It is time to let go of other energies; your own to heal. Trying to heal others doesn't help you. Practice achieving goals. You have to help you. Many [are] afraid to heal themselves.

Katherine: Why would they be afraid to heal themselves?

Angel: Not to heal themselves is to forget who they are. It's time to remember who they are. If only you knew who you are! You are attuning to who you are now. You are an amazing one. You are wonderful Being of Energy; you've tried to forget it. You have to give up those old beliefs about yourself. Are you forgetting you have come [here] to know who you are and to experience *more* of who you are? You have to feel that you are deserving of this experience. You have to remember that you came in to help other people and so as you are doing this. You must remember that you have to come in with a knowledge that you brought with you.

51

When you came in, you knew who you were and when you lived on the planet, you almost forgot who you were. That was again the choice of the whole nine-to-five experience. It isn't to forget but [rather the] goal was to participate and when you did that you would solely help others to hold the light. This time, it's time for you to create more light and again you came in to heal these old aspects, so you have to remember who you are now. You forgot but the time has come for you not to forget anymore. You have to help the Earth and to heal your own heart. It's time, it's time.

Katherine: Yes, it's time.

Angel: Now we are going to achieve this together. It's time for us all to achieve Ascension together. Have to remember who you are and who you came in with, who you came in to be. Who was that? Now is time to remember who you came to be, who you are going to be and who you are; what are you coming in to be.

Katherine: What is the best way to remember that?

Angel: The best way to remember? What is the best way to run? What's the best way to eat and sleep? What is the best way to do those things?

Katherine: Just to do them.

Angel: Well, you have to remember that it is not easy to achieve things without guidelines. You are achievers already. My, you have held on to others' beliefs. How nice that others want to tell you what to do, but now is your time to say how to achieve things. You have to tell yourself. You've got to listen to your own Self.

Krista: I don't know if I'm being challenged but a part of me is really mad at them. I don't know why. I don't want them taking over. I don't know if it's my ego but I don't want them taking over this thing —

Katherine: It's all right.

Krista: — Or ruining my life.

Katherine: That's your ego, asserting itself. It's all right. You are the one in charge. Kodoish, Kodoish, Kodoish, Adonai Tsebayoth. Holy, holy, holy is the Lord God of Hosts.

Krista: I get so tired when I do this.

Katherine: It's all right, it's energy; you are acclimating to the new energies.

Krista: Thank you. I'll lay down the whole time.

Orion Council: We have to say that it is not easy for us to talk with the channel when the channel is not feeling her cooperation. It is not easy for us to talk when not cooperating.

Katherine: Why do you think she is angry? Is that her ego kicking up?

Orion Council: Of course. It is ego.

Katherine: Interfering?

Orion Council: Yes-*ah*.

Katherine: Feeling threatened?

Orion Council: Yes-*ah*.

Katherine: Feeling it will be destroyed?

Orion Council: Yes-*ah*.

Katherine: I'll try to help her with that.

Orion Council: Please-*ah*.

Katherine: The ego has a special job, to keep the body safe.

Orion Council: Right. It is the wanting to have the control, of the experience. Wanting control of all experience in this life time.

Katherine: That's not its proper job, is it?

Orion Council: Not at all. Expansion is the purpose of your lifetime. Not to stay in a box.

Katherine: What do you think is something that would soothe the ego, or is it something just to be ignored?

Orion Council: Both. You can try to soothe the ego [by] using affirmations. Saying you are safe and so on. That you will be safe while expanding, for example.

Katherine: Oh, thank you. Krista, do you hear that? You are safe to expand. It is safe for you to expand. That resistance, is it lessening now?

Orion Council: Yes.

Katherine: Well, with whom do we have the pleasure of —

Orion Council: Council of Orion, here.

Katherine: I thought so. It's a different one, today.

Orion Council: Many of us, here.

Katherine: Eight?

Orion Council: Ten of us, here. Ten of us here.

Katherine: Who are the other two?

Orion Council (Emphatically): One of us is the training officer.

Katherine: Hello, again.

Orion Council: Heh, heh, heh. Training officer is wanting this experience to be a profound one. We are wanting you all to feel this sensation that we bring in: positive vibrations from Orion energy. It is time for all of you to focus on the light within yourselves. You are made of light, you are made of light. When humans forget who they are, they walk in darkness. They do not know the light is there. All you must do is turn on the light. That is your job, simply to turn on the light where others cannot see. Others cannot see. Are you going to help the others? Maybe some of them.

Katherine: Yes, if they are wanting.

Orion Council: They will want, but they do not know yet that they want. They are having trouble because they have egos as well. Egos distract from the love. Egos want conditional love, [others] do not understand that love is so much greater than what they show in the movies.

Katherine: Is it possible to experience unconditional love while in this body?

Orion Council: Of course. If you have an animal, you will feel that love. You take animals because you love to give love, you see. You love to give love to animals and animals give love to you, whether you like it or not. They are constantly giving their love to you. How can you not feel that unconditional love?

Katherine: We humans have a rather limited understanding of love, I think.

Orion Council: Yes. Many of you are not remembering that you are made of love, light...So afraid to express this love to others, afraid of being left alone, afraid of forgetting who you are. You think when you become a loving being, you will leave yourself out of the equation. Who will love you? [Giving example] It's not fair to love others if they don't love you back: that is conditional love. You give love and you expect it to come back, but you will love with your heart freely when you focus on the light within other people, as well. That love is felt within them.

When you realize and you have the awakened sense of their lightness, that is opening their eyes when you treat them as they deserve to be treated. Everyone has their own experience. It is like waiting for all to gather around this speaker. It is like [a] speech, when you wait for others to come listen. You come rushing to the front of the podium and others take longer because they see all the other ones and then they come. It's not overnight, but when you are focusing on the light, you will notice what happens. Many people will begin to see this energy and they will appreciate it, recognize it, they will gather around it in curiosity. "What is this new thing? Why am I feeling so good when I am reading this text? Why am I enjoying this spoken message so much? It feels so different from those other energies that I saw on the TV. This is a love message, here. I love this book. I love this author. Oh my, I feel so good when I read this book. It makes sense to me, now. I open my eyes to the love of light. I open my eyes to love of God. I am awake now. I am Creator of my life! I am awake now! I am awake!" How many will come together when they find out they are all a part of the same experience — they are all in this energy of Ascension. They are all part of something vast. It is that "thing" that brings them together, you see.

Katherine: Yes. May I ask you a question? I'm a little confused about the teaching that everything outside of us is a reflection of what's inside of us.

Orion Council: It is correct, but you have to understand that when you are focusing light on other people, they are focusing it back to you, too. You have to forget about their reactions to you. You have to remember if you focus light, that is what is helping other people. You have to forget that they will have their reactions to you. It's not important how they react to you when you have given in a love energy.

Katherine: You are saying that their reaction has nothing to do with us? That our job is to just focus the light?

Orion Council: Yes, and you will have a positive experience, exchange. When you focus the love in other people they will feel that.

Katherine: But we must just let go, at that point of how they —

Orion Council: You must give in love. That's it. You can live your lives loving others and yourself. So take your time and love others when you can.

Katherine: Yes, but doesn't it start with loving one's self?

Orion Council: Perhaps it is better to forget what they think of you. Perhaps it is better to forget their opinions of you and others. What does it matter what they are thinking? You are the one who is thinking.

Katherine: Isn't that another aspect of the ego? Wondering if they will approve?

Orion Council: This time you must remember that to love another is to heal yourself, too. In your loving of others, you are healing a part of yourself that needs love.

Katherine: Can you elaborate on that a bit, please?

Orion Council: When you are loving other ones, you are remembering you are all made of love. That heals a part of you that needs to be healed. When you are loving another one, you are seeing that you are capable of giving this love and so in turn, you are able to give it to yourselves.

Katherine: Okay, thank you.

Orion Council: You can do it.

Katherine: Could you explain what aspects are?

Orion Council: Yes, there are many aspects that are wanting to be expressed now. Those aspects are taking their time but they are rising to the surface of your waking experience. They are the soul wanting to express itself more in this physical reality. Aspects are gathering kind of like these particles in a tree. They are like those leaves on the tree that want to bud, have flowers, you see. That is what the soul is like. It is like a tree. The aspects are like the flowers and the leaves of the tree. Aspects are the part of the soul that wants to be expressed. Infinite possibilities the soul has, you see. So it is, ah, quite excited for you now. The soul is wanting expansion more than ever before. The possibilities now are quite immense. It is endless, you see. Your waking self gets to decide what you want to do and you have the ego as well, so, what will you do with this opportunity now that you have it?

Katherine: Is there an infinite number of aspects?

Orion Council: They are like the budding particles that want expression. They want realization. They want your waking mind to realize they are there. They are like a hermit [crab] coming out of a shell. It is like the bud of a flower, wanting to express itself. It wants to show what it can do.

Katherine: Are these aspects carried from life to life experience?

Orion Council: They are kind of like those passing over through the dimensions. They are these energies from other dimensions. When you are a soul, you are probably not so aware of these other aspects. When you are in this physical reality, you are not aware of those other interdimensional aspects. They are interdimensional aspects. They have to be realized in order to manifest. So, you can tap into them when you're driven to change this time of your life. You will experience these aspects while you are changing your experience. You have to want to change your experience, then a soldier will come through, or a maker of light will come through, a helping hand will come through. A challenging time will prepare you for these new aspects to come through.

Katherine: I understand. You used the word "tapping." Is it possible for us to draw upon an aspect that we would *want* to express at that time?

Orion Council: You have so many that it is like a library.

Katherine: Is it possible, using your analogy of a library, to get a particular "book" on a particular "shelf" on a subject we want to express?

Orion Council: Yes, that is right. Now you've got it.

Katherine: [One of] the Council said to me a day or two ago, "Your soul is a painter." I had the feeling that they were referring to an aspect of the soul.

Orion Council: That's right. You were a painter once but you have to remember that you can do anything when you are painting. You can paint anything you want to, so, it has two meanings. This time you are not painting, you are training others to "paint."

Katherine: So just for clarification: if I or if Krista would want to draw upon an aspect that is bursting with confidence or a powerful, assertive presence, let's say, is it possible to draw upon that energy from that aspect for expression? Is that how it works?

Orion Council: It is a training time. Having to say that you have to train others to become what you have become.

Katherine: Are the angels with us now?

Orion Council: Yes.

Katherine: Is it okay to welcome our angels in?

Orion Council: No. Ha, ha, ha, ha! Joking.

Katherine: They requested last night to be asked in and I would like to invite them in.

Krista: Mom, it's your curiosity or your questioning that draws in their energy.

Katherine: Well, that's what the training officer was talking about.

Krista: But now I'm feeling tired again. I feel like I want to fall over; like I have no energy to sit up. I feel so like putty right now; I just want to lie down.

Katherine: Lie down, then. They said that you are acclimating to new energies.

Krista (Laying down): I can tell it's right! Oh, it's so comfortable! You're right. That's what it is. And you're calling in the angels, oh my God. That's cool, though. You can write a book about angels. What dimensions are they on? Okay...

Orion Council: Yes. Why do you all ask us these things? They are training you now, to help others. You must understand that when you are loving other people, others will feel this energy. You cannot see the love. Some make songs, you see it in their eyes, but you cannot see the love physically. Yes, it is felt.

Katherine: We see the expression of love, in nature.

Orion Council: Yes. Love is in many forms.

Katherine: Would you like to talk about the different forms?

Orion Council: There is love energy here, today. Energies are here, today.

Katherine: Welcome. You are welcome to share with us.

Orion Council: It's time for training. When you are focusing your energies, many come to listen to this exchange.

Katherine: I would like to say hello to everyone assembled.

Orion Council: Many energies here now. It is time for us to say today that you have to remember that this exchange is not to frighten you. Not frighten. This is the Council of Orion, your friends. It's our turn to speak with you. So many energies here are listening to us, they are wanting to participate but it is our turn. So what do you want to talk about?

Katherine: Are all eight of you —

Orion Council: Ten Council members.

Katherine: Oh, including the training officer.

Orion Council: Correct.

Katherine: Sorry, I didn't mean to leave you out.

Orion Council: That's okay.

Katherine: Who is the tenth?

(Slow speech): Angel . .Being . .of . .Light . .The . .Angel of Mercy. Tree—tree—treat, treat your friends with love. Angel wants you to treat your friends with love.

Katherine: Yes.

Angel: Angel of Uriel.

Katherine: Uriel?!

Angel (Very softly): Uriel. Angel of Mercy. Angel of Uriel. God's second tr- tr...trying to help her. Can you help her? Angel of Quieting the Mind. Angel creating this arrangement. Angel of Fortunate...wait, wait. Angel of...wait...Krista is not feeling the energy of Uriel quite right.

Katherine (Gently): Relax, Krista, relax.

Angel: Why not friendship with angels? Can you feel these energies? Angel of Uriel here. Uriel.

Katherine: Uriel, welcome.

Angel: Uriel is here...Hi.

Katherine: Welcome!

Angel: Darling *darlings*. Angel of Uriel here.

Katherine (Weeping with emotion): Hello...

Angel: Goodness, it's so friendship here. It's your friends on this side. We are your friends; it's our pleasure to speak with you. Well, it's time for us to say you're a friend to All-That-Is.

Katherine: Thank you.

Angel: You are such a wonderful gal. You are a good person, you have the heart of gold. You and your daughter are golden light of appreciation. It's time for this friendship to blossom: your friendship with yourself; your Higher Self.

Katherine: Yes, yes.

Angel: Good. Uriel is a friend saying you have to love your own Self. Uriel is a friend of you. It's a fine day today.

Katherine: What are some ways to love one's self?

Angel: Well you know you have this help, you see. You could not be a great being without so many helpers wanting to help you. That means you are something quite good. You are someone quite appreciated in creation. You are someone with quite a bright light, you see. This is why all of us want to help you. You're light is shining so brightly. That's why we are here to help you. Have to say that Krista is a fine young lady.

Katherine: Yes, she is.

Angel: Having to help others is the task of both of you; that's all there is to do. You have to help them remember their sovereignty. Yes?

Katherine: They *are* sovereign.

Angel: Yes.

Katherine: Isn't it so, that everyone is a bright light?

Angel: Yes. *All* are bright lights. All are not so afraid like you two can be, but they are the ones who are trying to change the world now, not focused on the Spirit Life: they are focused on job for changing the world. Many are wanting to change the world but they are not focused on their spiritual selves. That is *your* job, to focus on the spiritual Self. You are the ones to discuss it, you see. Many have no opportunities to discuss it, for they do not create them. They are focused on their jobs that will help the Earth to change. All is well. That's why you all don't have the same jobs, you see. Makes sense, yes? Doesn't it?

Katherine: All is in Divine Order.

Angel: That's right.

Katherine: We all have our different jobs to do. We chose them, did we not, when coming into this Earthly experience?

Angel: That is true.

Katherine: I just want to keep my ego in check.

Angel: You have no ego problems, Katherine. You are just a fine woman, you are. No problem.

Katherine: Thank you.

Angel: This is our message, so friendships with the angels are possible, yes? Thank you for your help in this world. We are loving you now. Love you tomorrow as well. So it's nice seeing you smile, you're the lightworker, you are the Godsend. You are the brightest star. You are the Show-er of bright light. You are the princess of light. You have to forget the past and this time become who-you-are in this planet.

Katherine: Would you be able to help, or would Archangel Michael be able to help cut the cords?

Angel: Yes. His turn to talk. Archangels will talk, now.

Katherine: Thank you.

Angel: It's our pleasure.

Katherine: Thank you.

Krista: Wow! No wonder I felt so good. I didn't know there were Archangels in the room. When you talked about them, you asked for them. You asked for them!

Katherine (Chuckling): They said to ask for them, yesterday; I'm just following instructions.

Krista: How humble we are. We had this exchange and we're still very centered, not jumping off the walls. If I were eleven years old, I would be jumping off the walls.

Katherine: I think we're very grateful.

Krista: I think this is obviously natural for us because we're taking this as something totally normal.

Katherine: It is totally normal.

Krista: Yes. It's like shopping at the grocery store on Saturday.

Katherine: They said it would feel like the next logical step.

Krista: Okay, I think it's an angel coming in because I'm feeling so sleepy. It's such a high vibration. I feel like I'm drifting off into a dream state. Oh my goodness, I was thinking, "Which one is the Angel of Mercy?" Michael's Band of Mercy. Maybe they're merged together.

Katherine: I'm asking for Michael to step forward.

Krista: Okay; I think they're merging together but let's see. They do that you know, in orbs.

Archangel: So... So...That is why you are here, to be this free Spirit. You are the one who is changing the world. Yes, you are the free one.

Katherine: The free one trying to remember that they are free: Ehyeh Asher Ehyeh. I wanted to ask Archangel Michael for help.

Archangel Michael (Loudly): Well, you have it, now. One time you must ask only, and you are helped. [Ask] one time only. You are helped immediately. *Immediately!* Have to say thank you for your help. Can you remember to say thank you for your help, please?

Katherine: I will remember to say thank you.

Archangel Michael: Good, thank you.

Katherine: Thank you. And I have already asked you.

Archangel Michael: Yes, you have. It's done.

Katherine: Thank you. Thank you.

Archangel Michael: Welcome.

Katherine: Thank you.

Archangel Michael: Yes, you're welcome.

Katherine: Can you feel my thanks?

Archangel Michael: Yes. Well done, good job. Thank you, too. We are your friends, here. Heaven is wanting to help you.

Katherine: We want to fulfill what we came here to do.

Archangel Michael: Talk about us and that's fine. Only need to talk and you are doing your jobs.

Katherine: Are you referring to the book?

Archangel Michael: Angels. Yes, that too. Only need to discuss the angels and you are doing what you came to do. Why make it more difficult than that? You come up with these human intricacies that are unnecessary. You have fulfilled all that you came to do and simply by talking about us you are fulfilling your mission as a lightworker. What is so difficult about that?

Katherine: It just doesn't feel as if it is enough just to talk.

Archangel Michael: It does not? What do you think you are doing when you are talking about us to others?

Katherine: Oh, you meant to others. I didn't quite understand that.

Archangel Michael: Not to yourself, certainly. Why only to yourself? Are you a hermit?

Katherine: No.

Archangel Michael: No, that's correct, so when you are discussing our energies with others that is why you have come. And so you are fulfilling your mission on this planet. That's what you have to do. I Am Michael.

Katherine: Will you please help us with this book?

Archangel Michael: Yes.

Katherine: Thank you, thank you.

Archangel Michael: Yes. You're welcome. Fine to see you here.

Katherine: And fine to speak with you.

Angel: Hi there. Too many angels here now.

Katherine: Who is this now?

Angel: Angel of Friendship.

Katherine: Welcome.

Angel: So many friends here, today. That's why we have come in, so you can talk with us.

Katherine: What is your work, Angel of Friendship?

Angel: To bring people together.

Katherine: Ah! That's such a blessing.

Angel: Why are you afraid of others? Silence is needed when you are focusing on this energy. You must focus your energy on the communication, not the ego. You are Divine, so remember it. You are Divine, remember it — stop crying so much. You're the Godhead, you're the one with the light shining for others. Now you have to say that you know you are love and light. Please say that.

Katherine: "I am love and light."

Angel: Yes. Now another angel, here.

Katherine: Welcome.

Angel: Silence is needed when you focus light within yourself, not the head.

Katherine: The heart.

Angel: Who are you?

Katherine: I'm Source expressing Itself.

Angel: So now that you know, next thing to do is what?

Katherine (Weeping with emotion): To express It. to let It through.

Angel: That's correct.

Katherine: Who is this now?

Angel: We are Metatron. It's time for you to stop crying and work. Okay. Stop crying and wipe your face. Ha, ha, ha, ha! You are the Godhead, here. You are the friendship of love and light, that is who you are.

Katherine: Thank you for saying that.

Angel of Metatron: Why don't you believe you are? Who said you are not? Why does it feel different when you talk to angels and why does it feel different when you read a book about angels? Why is it different? Why is it different when you talk to other people? Some just feel better than others. Why do you not believe that you are this love energy? Why do you not remember that?

Katherine: This damn conditioning.

Angel of Metatron: So what?

Katherine: I wish to release this conditioning.

Angel of Metatron: So what about them. Who cares?

Katherine: Metatron, may I ask you some questions, please?

Angel of Metatron: Yes.

Katherine: You know the studies that I'm involved in?

Angel of Metatron: Yes.

Katherine: Am I on track?

Angel of Metatron: Yes, next question. Keep it up.

Katherine: In part of the studies, I'm supposed to —

Angel of Metatron: Why are you trying to work out the system when you are just asked to live it? And love it? You are trying to figure out like engineers, how it all works. You are forgetting to live it. Live it. Go out in the world and live it. You have to! You have to. You have to reach your hand to others. You have to help them. Please. Angels asking you now to help others. Will you do that?

Katherine: Yes.

Angel of Metatron: Please, please. Angels are asking you, please. Please help. Please help.

Katherine: Yes, yes. This book should help.

Angel of Metatron: It will help.

Katherine: Metatron?

Angel of Metatron: Yes?

Katherine: In this program we are instructed to ask for your light or connect with your light.

Angel of Metatron: Fine. You have many, many angels to connect with. When you focus on one it is only one vibration.

Katherine: Is it all the same vibration?

Angel of Metatron: It is only one vibration out of many.

Katherine: Is it right to ask for that?

Angel of Metatron: What do you mean, "is it right?" Who says it is not? Your choices are your own.

Katherine: It just seems a little lazy.

Angel of Metatron: Why is it lazy to ask for help? Why can't you request it of others, if it is our job? We do not have human egos, you see. That is quite a good choice to ask for help.

Katherine: For light, simply more light, more light.

Angel of Metatron: That's what you have to do. Create more light here. Why are you stepping back?

Katherine: I won't step back.

Angel of Metatron: This time we will succeed.

Katherine: We will.

Angel of Metatron: Yes. This time around, there is no room for failure.

Katherine: That's very encouraging, thank you for sharing that.

Angel of Metatron: You're welcome. Now, you need to rest and then have another session with us.

Katherine: All right. Will you come in or will we need to call you?

Angel of Metatron: Nice try. We will be here.

Katherine: Thank you.

Angel of Metatron: You're welcome.

Katherine: We appreciate you all and your love. Thank you. Good bye.

Angel of Metatron: Good bye.

Session 5

Krista: I want know who's in the room.

Katherine: All right, let's start with that.

Orion Council: So many of us here in the room, now.

Katherine: Welcome.

Orion Council: So many are wanting to talk with you. Can you see the energy lined up? Aligned energies. All right. It is time to talk with you. Many of us, here.

Katherine (Joking): Is there space to sit down?

Orion Council: Many of us, no space. Only room to float about. Goodness! Cannot sit with you. So many taking up space. Oh, Katherine, it's nice to talk with you. Orion, here.

Katherine: Greetings, greetings.

Orion Council: You can discern between our energies, can you not?

Katherine: I believe I can.

Orion Council: Okay, okay. We are glad to talk with you. It's us here, Orion here. So many of us are wanting your friendship and that is up to you, whom you want to befriend. As you have noticed, there were many angels wanting to talk with you. So, you have the option in every moment to decide whom call in. So far we have made this connection with you because it is clear now and we would like to continue this discussion with you. And we would like to embark upon a new process of creation with you.

Katherine: That sounds wonderful.

Orion Council: Would you like that?

Katherine: Yes.

Orion Council: Wonderful, so, what can we all accomplish together? So many of us are here. So many are wanting your help. So many are glad that you exist. How does that make you feel as a Creator? Do you know that you have the opportunity to bring in more light to this Planet Earth? Do you know how that feels for us, for everyone on this side? Do you know how it feels, to be creating for All-That-Is? Do you know how good that feels? For us, for everyone on this side?

Katherine: Yes, it's really thrilling.

Orion Council: Yes, you are quite an amazing Creator. You are fascinating and your ability to heal others is quite strong, you see. You have that gift: to heal people. Keeper [Krista] is saying that you are not healing, you are helping them to heal. That's correct, but as a healer in this duality, this dualistic experience you are in, you are the one who is basically thought of as a healer. The other ones will look and they do want a fix and that is fine, because it's set up that way. When you go to the store you get some food. That's how it's set up.

Katherine: That's a different energy signature that came in just now.

Orion Council: Quite right.

Katherine: Also the Council?

Orion Council: Yes. "Mother." Hello. Now, what would you like to discuss?

Katherine: The book actually; Krista had some very specific questions.

Orion Council: Well, okay. It's time to discuss your project, yes? Well, this book will be quite a fascinating one. You are wondering what topics to write about, and the topics will be wonderful topics. All of them.

Katherine: Are you going to help us with that?

Orion Council: Of course we will. We are your helpers. What else would we do? Float around in the room with you?

(Laughter)

Orion Council: Yes, you know that it will be wonderful. You are sensing the prospects, the possibility. You are sensing the possible outcome of this project. That's your excitement, bubbling inside. You are feeling into the possibility of actually having your own book. Can you believe it? To have your name, it will have your address, *no, no, no.*

(Laughter)

Orion Council: It will have much information for other people to look into and it would be respected as well. Well, how about money coming in with your spiritual assistance? How do you think that will feel for you as a Creator? It will feel magnificent. So, we would like to tell you that the possibilities of this book are endless. There are many different ways it could turn out. Because you are creating the book, you are working with mass consciousness, in a sense. You are molding the opportunities that exist, because of this. A chain of reaction, almost, is what would basically happen if you were to publish such a text. There would be a chain of reactions, as is with all things that are created. If you have a painting, a painter will sell the painting. The painting has its own history and painters are studied, even. Painting will be maintained by museums. Ah, the possibilities are endless for something that you once create. Don't think that it's over now, once you do.

Katherine: One question that Krista had was will you —

Orion Council: Participation in the project? You must take one step at a time because it's this time [that] we need to discuss what we want first, before we "jump the gun," as you say. We must decide what is important and what makes you feel joy.

Katherine: Is that to be the guiding light?

Orion Council: Yes, of course. It's the only way to go. The joyful path is the only way to go. Once you create this, you are opening up the possibilities. You will be onto the next thing, the next project. It's one fun thing to do. So, when you are focusing on this, what are the fun topics? What would you like to discuss? What do you want to write about? You will feel the passion when you are beginning to transcribe the text. When you are typing the words, you will know which words you prefer to type. You will figure out what you want. Now is not the time for a huge list.

Now you must just take one step at a time. See what feels right for you.

Katherine: You also said, a few days ago, the first step is learn about the publishing.

Orion Council: Yes, you must do some research. It is, of course, involved and you must look into companies. Possibilities are endless. Many are now beginning to focus on these New Age topics, as you say. The timing is perfect for this project. The possibilities are endless.

Katherine: I think we also need to think about to whom we are directing —

Orion Council: Well, it is not so important because the publishing company will know what to focus on when working with the original text. You may need to add a chapter or a paragraph or a whole section or take out some parts. This is why it is good to have lots of material, you see.

Katherine: That is very true. But what I was thinking was about the audience.

Orion Council: Are you writing for them or for yourself? Well, you do want to consider [them] but it's not as important as what makes you happy.

Katherine: I was thinking about writing for adults versus writing for children.

Orion Council: It will come later for the children. A very good question nonetheless. We apologize for the interruption. You had a very valid question.

Katherine: Thank you, that's quite all right.

Orion Council: Many wanting to speak with you tonight. Are you prepared?

Katherine: Yes.

Orion Council: Krista talks about the abundance of the universe and how it gets better all the time. Feeling excited about the book and channeling. So many of us wanting to talk with you tonight. Can you feel the energies here? There are many in line. Orion here, but many others wanting to talk with you. "Channel feeling very clear," she says, tonight. Finally appreciating herself, makeups and all. Okay, very funny. Not so funny. Channel [Krista] does not like us making fun of her choices.

(Another energy): It's our turn now. We have to help you. You are fine woman, Katherine. It is us, angels. Angels are here tonight. We love you. You are wonderful. Angels of White Light, here.

Katherine: Welcome, angels.

Angels: Thank you. Nice to see you. My, you are a fine woman. It's — how do we say it — "pretty nice" to see you. We are the ones who came to communicate with you. It's our turn to be with you, tonight. It's our turn. Well done, with the other angels. Creating with the angels. Many need to work with their angels. Many have forgotten their angels. We are imparting energies to you. You are not forgetting us, now. We have to help you, as well. You are a magnificent Creator in front of us. Many of us are here and we are wanting to befriend you.

Katherine: Welcome, welcome.

Angels: Many angels here. Many angels here. Do you remember us?

Katherine: Yes.

Angels: Remember angels, loving angels. When you were born there were angels, when you die there are angels. You are seeing us. Angels want to be your friend. Angels want to help you. We can do many things. We can do healing with you. Do you want to heal with us?

Katherine: Indeed!

Angels: You can do it, with us.

Katherine: By just asking?

Angels: Well, yes. You can do that if you want to do it. Well, can you ask us, please? We can help you with healing energies. It's time to forget the old things that have hurt you. You have to help yourself. You have to welcome your angels in.

Katherine: Just by invoking, is that enough?

Angels: Yes. That is enough. Yes.

Katherine: Archangel Michael said to ask only once and it is done.

Angels: Yes. Angel of Mercy is the Heavenly Soldier. It's done when you ask for it to happen.

Katherine: What of Archangel Ariel?

Angels: Ariel is away--*ting*.

Katherine: Ha, ha, very tricky.

Archangel Ariel: Ha, ha, ha! Too bad you have forgotten Ariel.

Katherine: I have not!

Archangel Ariel: You are not forgetting Ariel, are you?

Katherine: Never!

Archangel Ariel: Ariel is training Krista.

Katherine: Wonderful.

Archangel Ariel: You have to remember your connection with all of us. You are going places, Katherine.

Katherine: Literally?

Archangel Ariel: Well, what do you think we meant? Are you trying to go somewhere or not? You have to focus the energy on that which you want first, of course. In the past you've forgotten your connection. At times, when times have been rough you did not ask for angels to help you. That's all right, because that was a learning process. Now you know that you are always having your angels by your side. You are dreaming of us, sometimes. When you are sleeping, sometimes you will notice we will pop in to say hello. You are ready for the next move.

Katherine: What will that be?

Archangel Ariel: Well, you have very thin skin when it comes to making decisions, sometimes. Others are going to do what they want to do, always. You have not really considered what you want to do. You are beginning to remember that in a sense, it is all about you. You have forgotten that Divine Right that you have to yourself, to be your own master, to be an island of compassion, yet an island of grace and understanding as well. You are a Light Being that needs to plant its feet in the soil. You are wanting to feel that light within you. That light is shining, it is a very bright light. You just need to focus the energies on the things that you are wanting. Your light will draw them in, especially when you activate those light quotients in those experiences, objects, people or things. Those things are immediately drawn to you in the ethers. It's up to you whether you want to magnify that attractive quality or not. You are the one who is in the control seat.

Katherine: When you say to focus the light on the things that you want, is it as simple as just thinking about those things?

Archangel Ariel: You feel emotion when thinking about those things.

Katherine: So, it is just thought and feeling combined.

Archangel Ariel: Of course.

Katherine: That's flowing the light in some direction?

Archangel Ariel: Yes.

Katherine: Thank you.

Archangel Ariel: Of course.

Katherine: The imagination is — that a very valid way? Getting a picture, adding the feeling to that picture, infusing it with the feeling of joy and excitement and whatever qualities — is that correct?

Archangel Ariel: When you find the right picture, you will know. If you feel excitement, searching for a picture, you will know that is the path. You will be led to the right things. It only takes a few minutes to focus on that which you want for yourself. Others will constantly tell you what they want. And are your ears open to that or to what you are wanting for yourself? Other people will always have their own agendas. There are no bad people, of course, but these other ones are Creators as well. So, it is beautiful when Creators come together for a common cause. However, they are creating their own separate ways as well.

Katherine: Yes. Krista was concerned about her friend and about getting married and living in New York.

Archangel Ariel: He has his own agenda as well. He is a Creator as well. He is the one who wants to befriend other women, too. It's not fair to only belong to one person. There are many people in the world, wanting to connect with each other at this time. We must allow for this to happen, because the like-minded individuals will come together. That is what is happening on the planet now.

Katherine: Like-minded individuals?

Archangel Ariel: Yes. They are connecting.

Katherine: This is wonderful.

Archangel Ariel: Why do so many people want to travel? They are wanting to connect with like-minded individuals. So many changes are happening, now. You are seeing this in the news, you are seeing this all over: in your personal life and experiences in yourself. So it has come for all of us to raise the energy of the planet and that means that many of us will be moving to, relocating to, other places — in clusters, almost. They will be enjoying that energy of groups. That is happening in the New Age. Groups will form. Some you will resonate more than with others. You may belong to many groups. All groups will serve certain purposes. When you are feeling discord, it is because one of your aspects is either too loud or you are not paying attention to your own needs. Some of those energies are uncalled for. Some of those energies are too loud, ego-ridden, ego-based beliefs, and there are also other aspects that need to calm down the aspects that do not serve the highest good. You need to check in, at times, and ask your Higher Self, "Is this for the highest good, when I continue my painting career?" for example. We like that reference because many of you know who painters are. Many paint.

Katherine: I like that idea about clusters of like-minded people. Is it also true that one need not necessarily travel to find such a group? Maybe it is right around the corner from where they currently are?

Archangel Ariel: That is also quite possible. But many will be moving in the future.

Katherine: When you say future, do you mean near —

Archangel Ariel: In the next 20 or so years.

Katherine: Of course, we humans have a very different perspective of time. By the way, is it accurate to say that time is compressing into the single "now" moment?

Archangel Ariel: Well, time needs to catch up with what's happening on the planet. You are all so rapidly evolving that time needs to catch up. You have the illusion that time dissipates. You have the illusion that time is a constant streaming flow, when you are actually quantum leaping at times. You are quantum leaping ahead and back. You are fluctuating between past and future potentials, constantly. So therefore, you are not in a time system, you are outside of the time system when you are deliberately focusing your energies on future events. But, of course, your experience is a continual process. Of course there is no such thing, but that linear behavior is what keeps you all aligned to the mass consciousness. You must refer to points in time to have a common understanding of what is going on.

Katherine: To change the subject slightly, today I heard a news report *(Ed. note: regarding Japan's 3/11/11 earthquake and tsunami)* about the radiation in Japan spreading to Hawaii in the next two weeks, and then parts of California and Washington State and —

Archangel Ariel: And hurricanes and tornadoes, yes, yes, yes.

Katherine: Is this fear-mongering or —

Archangel Ariel: Well, Earth changes as you know, are inevitable. They are bound to happen. And as many of your Orion friends have said, they are timed events. So when you have an eruption on one side of the planet you must balance the act. Perhaps the water level goes down on one side of the world; it must be balanced. Perhaps there is old, pent-up energy that needs to be released. You will have an eruption. It is all a balancing act. Finally, Earth is shifting its focus. There are many parts of your Earth that are wanting to be expressed now. It is why ages come and go. All of you have collectively asked for a more benevolent future — the majority — so it must happen. If you are all wanting a more benevolent reality, you must release that which is not as benevolent. So, one by one, earthquakes happen. It is like the chills. When you are feverish, you have the chills. It is almost a shaking off of the old: burning up that which is no longer needed. These Earth changes are inevitable. They will happen in many different places. When the brave ones pass, they will be celebrated on the Other Side. They are going to have the best party there has ever been in creation. Many of you fear the death process but we tell you that nothing is greater than to pass over. Nothing feels as good. Of course, love and joy are up there on the same feeling, but it is [like returning], as if you have been away from family that loves you, for so long.

Katherine: It is a Homecoming.

Archangel Ariel: Yes. If you thought Krista's flowers were nice, wait till you die.

Katherine: She sent those to me, I'm sure.

(Ed. note: on the day that Katherine learned of her pregnancy, she discovered a large bouquet of flowers in an empty gym locker that she had selected at random, as she was changing her clothes for a sports event.)

Archangel Ariel: Well, can we tell you or shall you keep on guessing?

Katherine: Please, tell me about it.

Archangel Ariel: It was a set-up, you see. There were many helping this event. You were wanting to experience

86

something so grand [that] you brought in an Energy to you and it assisted you in this decision you had made.

Katherine: Am I correct in assuming it was the energy of my child, Krista?

Archangel Ariel: Well, Krista was there, watching it happen. You were wondering where to go. The Energy directed you nicely, to go to the right place at the right time; a Benevolent Energy. Krista was there.

Katherine: Are you saying there was a separate, Benevolent Energy and Krista was a part of it?

Archangel Ariel: Yes, correct.

Katherine: Oh, I see. So what was the Benevolent Energy?

Archangel Ariel: Simply a Benevolent Being, wanting to help.

Katherine: Well, I would like to thank that Being for helping.

Archangel Ariel: It is done.

Katherine: This would be something I would like to include in our book.

Archangel Ariel: You may.

Katherine: I'd like to start with a prayer: Kodoish, Kodoish, Kodoish, Adonai Tsebayoth.

Krista: Wow!

Orion Council: It is good. Yes, doing well. You are very good at the praying.

Katherine: Thank you.

Orion Council: Have you remembered to speak a language of light? You are doing that now; you are speaking that language of light. It probably has been a while but you are proficient in that language, Katherine.

Katherine: Really?

Orion Council: Yes. You can learn this language but you have to forget what you are thinking about; it will come out of your mouth without thinking of it. You cannot think about it when you speak this language of light. That is why it is the hardest language.

Katherine: Krista has several questions for you, as I'm sure you already know.

Orion Council: We are prepared for these questions.

Katherine: May I start then? Is that okay?

Orion Council: Yes, you may.

Katherine: Have any from Orion taken on human form?

Orion Council: No.

Katherine: Do the Greys, Draconians, and Reptilians exist?

Orion Council: Well, hold on a moment. These are terms you humans have created for extraterrestrial beings. These are terms created by humans. Categories. What is a Grey? It is a type of alien classification by government. Andromedans are not aliens. Aliens are human-decided: what humans have decided them to be. There are many Light Beings all around.

Katherine: How are the beings from the Pleiades, Andromeda and so on, different from each other?

Orion Council: They have aspects that are their own kind for their own experiences outside of their own spaces.

Katherine: She wants to know why she is specifically channeling Orion?

Orion Council: Because the alignment of energies is correct; it is attractive in quality. We know she has focused on us and it has begun to be a link to our planetary system. We have come a long way and we are trying to attune to the Earthly energies. We are extremely interested in the human species. We are trying to accommodate on the planet; we are wanting communication. We are trying to eliminate things that are not helping in Ascension. We want to esteem those who have practiced spiritual practices. We are wanting to esteem those who have trained and who are wanting more of a universal connection. There are many who are not focused in this way but we are enjoying this energy and so we are enjoying this communication. It is only because of the need for our attention, that has brought us in. We are trying to create a new kind of dynamic on Earth which includes contact and so on. We are wanting to communicate with more human beings. We are wanting to have more of a training on Earth.

Katherine: Based on what you just said about reaching more humans, what do you think of the idea of Krista speaking before audiences; channeling before audiences?

Orion Council: It's a good idea because it will capture many peoples' attention. It takes a lot of skill to speak to people but she can do this if she wants to. It's not easy but it can be done. You only have to intend for such a gathering and it will happen.

Katherine: Krista asks if she has lived many lives on Sirius?

Orion Council: That is also an interesting facility. It is one used for human experience. Before you become a human, you can live in Sirius and attune to the energies of Earth. It's not as intense, not as dense as Earth. It's so etheric, it is. Etheric.

Katherine: Is the same true of the Pleiades?

Orion Council: That is a brotherly planet. It is for your brothers of light. They have many drummers who are coming in to play here. Drummers and such artists come from that place. Musical beings and artists are very Pleiadian. That is a place like your planet; not so different but more art and beautiful lifestyle.

Katherine: Ah, lovely! Are there humans living on Earth who are from Orion?

Orion Council: Many are from Orion but they are not humans. Orion visitors are etheric ones. Like Sirius ones. Orion is like those. Well, it is something quite unusual.

Katherine: She asks about energy from space vehicles; the energy from space ships.

Orion Council: They are all over the place. They are simply devices, intergalactic devices. So many are wanting communication. They are using these, creating training all over. Wanting assessment of these new places; wanting protection for themselves but wanting to assess – being careful. So create a space ship, then you can explore.

Katherine: And they land?

Orion Council: Yes, they can land on land if they want to or use tools to stay in the air.

Katherine: I was told that the place that I go to in Arkansas is a special place with many portals. What of portals?

Orion Council: It is not for you, it is for others coming in. You have opportunity to ask us; your class will be stimulating. We'll tell you about these things. Portals are for intergalactic community to attune to your home planet energy. It's like a safe place for us to use to connect to Earth's energies.

Katherine: There is a writer who says that she connects with Pleiadian energy and offers attunements. Do you see value in that?

Orion Council: These attunements are causing a shift in your vibration. These are just the sort of distractions for your waking self — perfectly working — telling you to focus here and here and here.

Katherine: The attunements are to help us focus? So there's some value there but they're not necessary?

Orion Council: Well, it is all belief system, though: [if] you believe it is attuning to higher energies, you will feel that you have moved. Yes, all is well, they are used as tools for your Ascension. They are not something you must eat, like a special food but again you believe special foods are powerful.

Katherine: Everything goes back to belief, it seems.

Orion Council (Wryly): Yes, hard-to-find foods are always better for you.

Katherine (Bursts out laughing): Ha, ha, ha! Was that — that sounds like dry humor!

Orion Council: Well you call it what you want to call it. You are a very funny one.

Katherine: Well that last comment by you was hilarious! The hard to find ones are the ones we most value: the pricier, the more exotic, the more we crave it.

Orion Council: Of course, it is only logical.

Katherine: Human logic. If we believe it would grow another leg or something, would we get it?

Orion Council: Perhaps that, too.

Katherine: I guess that's why we have those who believe that they do not need to eat –that they only have to breathe. They are called "breatharians" and live on breath.

Orion Council: Yes. To believe such radical ideas, you must be focused in a community of like-minded individuals.

Katherine: Well, I believe it is also about the pleasure of eating. It's not just a matter of not needing to because you can live off of air and sunshine. We are in bodies for the physical experience, the enjoyment, too – is that not so?

Orion Council: Of course that is why.

Katherine: Well, I think I have asked all of Krista's questions. You do understand that in our human focus, we like to have names and we tend to categorize.

Orion Council: Yes, it is to point the finger at what you are talking about.

Krista: I'm really tired, Mom.

Katherine: Is it okay to ask one last question? Is Krista preparing for an out-of-body experience with this recurring fatigue?

Orion Council: She needs to hold on to what she came here to do. She must remember what she came here to do on Earth.

Session 7

Orion Council: We come in quickly today!

Katherine (Joking): Oh? Are you in a hurry?

Orion Council: No we have no time; literal. Are you feeling all right, today? Yes. Energies are fine today.

Katherine: Aren't energies always fine?

Orion Council: Well, some days they are perfect. You are not feeling quite yourself today, perhaps.

Katherine: Right, I'm still feeling a little out of sorts but it's okay.

Orion Council: We have to say that you are forgetting, sometimes, your own Self. And you must remember to focus light within yourself.

Katherine: Thank you for the reminder.

Orion Council: Okay. We say this because we know that it is part of the Ascension process, so we remind you quite frequently of this. You know that the light is focused within at all times but when you are focusing your conscious self in this way, you are bringing in more of this light quotient that you are, each time you focus the energy within, you see. So holding that conscious feeling and thought is what is bringing in more of the light quotient, yes? So we are trying to explain how this happens. It's a part of the creative process of who you are and what you are coming into being. You are coming into being! You are coming into being. Yes, okay, so, when you begin to come into being you are the one true Creator of your life. Helping the Earth is part of your purpose. You came and you said that you would help Earth. That was your promise as a Being of Light. For many ask, "What's my purpose?" So, we tell all it is to help Earth.

Katherine: What are some ways of helping Earth?

Orion Council: Meditating on what is good for Earth. Meditating on what is good for Gaia. We need people to focus the light on Gaia because that is your home; your second home.

Katherine: Yes. That feels very good.

Orion Council: It's time for us to discuss the Ascension process. You are focusing light on Gaia, but that means you are focusing on your selves as well. When you do this, the energies are immense. You become a more powerful Creator, you see, when you are focusing on this personal energy that you have. That is why healing works sometimes, because the presentation of the healer is quite believable. The healed person goes to the healer and the healer says "I can help you." It works because of the belief in their power. Although it is always self-healing, this belief is so strong, that it works. That is how everything works. Beliefs are ingrained in your minds from past lives, as well. So, unworthy feelings are from many lifetimes ago. All right, but now we must tell you to hold the light, as if you are focusing on candlelight, says Keeper [Krista]. You have to remember, this light is who you are. You are light, you are light, you are light. You know this, but others do not remember they are light. They have to know this, that they are light.

Katherine: It's essential.

Orion Council: Yes. What is it you are wanting to ask us today? Keeper [Krista] wants to know about us, but what do you want to know about us, Katherine?

Katherine: I would like to ask about everything being outside of ourselves. Meaning, that our consciousness is not within, but consciousness is without. Consciousness is ubiquitous, it is everywhere. But it is, reflected on the outside —

Orion Council: Outer world? Your thought processes, you mean?

Katherine: Is it accurate to say that all is happening within consciousness, from a human standpoint? Meaning, we are the center of our universe?

Orion Council: Many are wanting to help you with your questions. Many are wanting to help you, now.

Katherine: Yes, please help with this clarification of within and without. As above, so below, as within, so without.

Krista: Mom, they're shifting and I feel like I have to take a break. They were changing.

(Break)

Orion Council: My, it was easy to come in, today. Yes, well, such a bright channel, today. Well done. We have to tell you about your question about focusing light and are you consciousness always. Is that your question, are you always consciousness?

Katherine: No, I do believe we are always consciousness. What else would we be?

Orion Council: Are we in a sea of consciousness? Of course. It is all consciousness, it is something intangible. You cannot grasp exactly what "What It Is," is. You are wondering what is, Is? So, we are telling you, It is a myriad of things. There are quite many different levels of beingness and existence. So, this physical reality was one, conjured by God, you could say. And it was a thought, first. And it was accumulation of many participants, who wanted this experience. The senses had to be imagined first. It was quite complex, from your perspective. Many Creators were considering this possibility of having new sense perception. It was something that wasn't held upon in the other levels of existence. Many were holding on to this idea of a new sense perception, so this sense perception is what you are experiencing. Physicality — it's stepped down energy in a sense — because this level does not have those opportunities that the other levels have. It was like moving in slow motion. It was moving so slowly that we could not understand why anyone would want such a thing, but it was necessary for other levels of existence, other training purposes. We have to sometimes hold on to these old creations. Old creations were necessary to your experience — older creations.

Krista (Interjects): Mom, I don't know what they're talking about.

Katherine: What do you mean by "an older creation?"

Orion Council: We have to create something old for the planet. An old system. It had to be old. It was something you had practiced before you came into this lifetime. You had to have practiced on planets first before you could come into this lifetime.

Katherine: Are you referring to third dimension?

Orion Council: You had to have many 3-D experiences before you could raise the consciousness of the planet. You had to have those experiences because they formed a planetary alignment that would serve many in the future. You had to have an old system in your understanding of what was before you. Yes, in your minds, Keeper [Krista] says. You had to have an old, a past experience, to know that you were in a linear system. It was created, so of course there is no time but your minds tell you there was an "old," a past, a history because you need to believe you are in a linear system. You have to think that there is past and future, because that is a lesson for you. When you are able to understand you are beyond the time, you are beyond time: that is a lesson learned.

Katherine: Beautifully expressed, thank you very much.

Orion Council: Well, you are Creators! How else would you be existing on this planet if you were not a Creator? Even the rocks are Creators or part of Creators. Many are in this system and do not realize their true power. They [believe they] are so small and insignificant; it's quite surprising how many think they are so little, in your terms. Little is good: an ant knows its importance. We are not saying that you forgot that you were big, we are saying, at times you think you are little. It's duality, telling you that. Forget about that and you will ascend, if you are wanting Ascension.

Katherine: Simple but not easy.

Orion Council: Correct, but then again, whose perspective is that?

Katherine: My own.

Orion Council: Yes.

Katherine: Well, I think we are working diligently towards Ascension.

Orion Council: We are saying you have helped so many. You want to help, so we are reminding you for your book about what you can do.

Katherine: Yes, this is extremely helpful.

Orion Council: You are not required to step out of this existence, yet. You are not required. Many are wanting to step out, and will, but you are not required to do this. You are wanting physicality, now. Your soul wants physicality, now.

Katherine: Yes. Getting back to this discussion of consciousness being ubiquitous (everywhere and every-thing): of course, from our human perspective we have this sense of "inner," within our minds and spirits, within our feelings, and we have this sense of "without," outside of ourselves.

Orion Council: It is all a part of duality. You are wanting to transcend duality, are you? Perhaps you should rephrase the question. And, how does this question serve you now? How do you serve yourself when you know such a thing? We ask you because you are asking for the mechanics of this experience. Is that what you believe will help you transcend life? To understand how it works? Do you believe that more questions you come up with the more clever you are and thus you will be able to transcend intellectually? You will always have more questions, that is how we all are existing on this side. We have our questions. Nothing wrong with asking those questions. We are asking you, why you ask these questions?

Katherine: I don't believe that I can ascend intellectually; through the intellect.

Orion Council: Oh?

Katherine: I believe it is through the heart.

Orion Council: Well, do you believe that really?

Katherine: Well, maybe both, then.

Orion Council: Are you wanting Ascension? What are you wanting for yourself? Are you wanting Ascension? What does that mean, "Ascension?"

Katherine: That means, knowing who you really are.

Orion Council: Do you want to know who you really are?

Katherine: Yes, and it is not simply through my intellect. I already know intellectually who I am.

Orion Council: Well done, but why are you wanting Ascension? You want Ascension to know who you are. Is that correct?

Katherine: No, I want, I believe, Ascension is knowing, feeling, who —

Orion Council: You are wanting a heart-centered connection to God, perhaps. You are wanting to feel in your heart that you are God.

Katherine (Weeping): Yes, that is Ascension.

Orion Council: You have to release, so cry on. You must release so you can cry on. You are holding on to so much baggage in your heart. You have to release that old, old, material. You have been told you are not correct and unworthy. You are worthy and you are *right*. You are intending to create the love on this planet and who is to tell you that you cannot do that? Who told you that you can't? But they are wrong, as well. You have the choice in every moment. You have the choice: hold on/release; create/stay still; focus/be scattered. You have the choice, in every moment. Why do you hold on to those beliefs that do not serve you at all? Why do you feel insignificant when you are quite powerful? *Look at what you have created for yourself! Who are you? Who are you?*

Katherine (Softly): Creator.

Orion Council: Well, you do not believe you are Creator. We speak to you now like this. You still do not believe who you are. Why would we waste our time if you were insignificant? Why would we waste our time? There is no time, but, again, we are appreciating you immensely at this moment. You cannot see the angels in the room.

Katherine: Archangel Michael told me, "Dry your eyes!"

Orion Council: Well, because you are powerful one.

Katherine: I don't know if you understand, because as you told us a few days ago, you don't have the experience of feelings the way humans do. So it is, perhaps, difficult for you to understand that.

Orion Council: Correct. We come from a system where duality is not an issue. We are telling you our perspective of your situation. This is a different perspective. You are on that side of the veil, we are not so. We are being honest in what we are thinking.

Katherine: I understand that, but I'm saying to you that it is hard to answer your question about holding on to our baggage.

Orion Council: Why? We are wondering. Cannot understand why. Cannot understand.

Katherine: I think because it is difficult to release.

Orion Council: Why do you make it difficult? Why can it not be easy for you?

Katherine: Well, do you know what a ball of wax, is?

Orion Council: Yes.

Katherine: Okay, if you have, let's say this ball of wax was made up of many different colors and you wanted to take out only the red. It would be very difficult to separate the red out of all of the rest because it is a ball of wax.

Orion Council: Well, if you have created a ball of wax for yourself, it will be a ball of wax.

Katherine: Yes, and if that ball of wax is a creation over many, many so-called lifetimes and experiences, that makes it harder to separate out – in the current awareness of current life experience. I'm just using that as an example to illustrate why that is not so simple for humans to just release the —

Orion Council: You have the option to explain why it is difficult and you also have the option to release it. So, if you feel that you have balls of wax from the past, then you must focus on how to heal that belief. We are saying, you can simply change it and live a life of happiness. But that is our perspective, you see.

Katherine: How to change it?

Orion Council: You must know. You have to simply know who you are. You must walk around as if you were a light; a God of Light. And you have the symbolism and stories about what Gods are like. If you know how children imagine things, why do children like to play all the time? Why do they pretend all the time? Because they are tapping into those aspects of what it is like to play those roles. A God knows he or she is a mighty God and knows they are all powerful and in control of everything happening. The Gods [are] able to control weather, you see. "Kahuna," Krista says, "Kahunas, changing weather." You see, it's called magic, but the God is always a magician. A God has a power to alter other peoples' thinking. A God has the power to create, manifest into the physical world. Krista mentions Kahunas again. Creating from the etheric world something that is physical; a God does that. Something you are wanting, you think about and it comes into your experience; a God does that. The option to choose light from darkness; a God does that. Ability to sense what others are thinking; a God does that. Well, who is a God? A God creates universes. That's your next job but we are quantum leaping. You have the ability to simplify everything in your life and to see what you are doing and what you are capable of. You can focus your light energy however you want and intend to. So, there are many realms of existence and for many kinds of creations. You are in this physical one. You believe that you have a system of attachments to the past and if you believe that to be true, it will be. You are a God, you see. If you believe you are connected to the past, then you are connected to the past. Others believe – yes, others in Spirit, will tell you that you have to heal the past. Yes, you have to heal the past according to many spiritual beings. Who are you asking for advice? That's another question, you see. It is a game. You have your own beliefs. So we have our own beliefs. Many of us believe different things, you see. Simply because we are on this side of the veil does not mean we all agree about creation. You have the opportunity to change your perceptions at all times. So, we are telling you of your power and the possibilities for yourself. If you were healed by Jesus, do you believe Jesus would heal all of your past? We are saying that many on your Earth believe if they saw Jesus they would transcend life and ascend into Spirit. They have such a strong belief in the power of the Jesus Christ. We are saying that if you believe that you have that power within yourself, you would be quite an amazing light upon this planet. Many would flock to you for healing and advice. It is all a question of what you believe for yourself. We understand it is not easy to simply release, especially if you have patterns. We understand human beings live with patterns for behavior. We understand that you would hold patterns from other past lives. It makes sense. We are saying that you can simply release them, but you are saying it is not quite easy. You are saying that to hold on to the past is something natural that human beings do. So then it will be your experience, but if you are wanting to release the past, you must release the past or else hold on to it. Releasing the past is simply not holding on to those attributes that you no longer need for yourself. If they are patterns, they are patterns. If they are memories, they are memories. If they are beliefs, they are beliefs. If they are energies, they are energies. Everything, as you say, is consciousness. So, if a pattern is consciousness, can you release consciousness? Very good question. What is this ball of wax? Is it consciousness? Is it?

Katherine: No.

Orion Council: What is this ball of wax? Is it a physical ball? No. You are saying that you are holding onto many patterns. Indeed, you are holding onto many patterns. You believe that the way you function on this Earth is according to patterns and repetitive behavior. You believe that it is difficult to release a pattern that you have practiced for so many centuries. What is this pattern? Is it behavior? What is this energy? You say everything is energy, consciousness. Energy, ah, you think they are both separate? What is consciousness? What is thought? Is it energy?

Katherine: Yes.

Orion Council: All is energy. Well, is behavior, energy? Yes, of course it is. So, can you release energy? You believe you can release a blocked up energy. You believe you can release pent up anger. You believe you release these things. These are all concepts of the mind. You have a duality that you are working within. It is all a sea of energy, as you said this morning. A pattern of behavior; is that not

105

energy as well, repeated energy? Energy focused on, many times before?

Katherine: Yes. And although we use the term "release pent-up energy," "release blocked energy," would it be more accurate to say "redirecting," or "restructuring?"

Orion Council: Correct. If you feel that you are like a vessel that needs to be cleansed, then you would, yes, need to release old things for new. You would have to replace that container with new beliefs, which is a very wonderful idea for yourself because you could tell yourself new things. It is like you actually did with your cleaning. You make room for new things. So, if you have an empty house, you fill it up with furniture. If you want a new couch you have to get rid of the old couch. It makes sense in your minds. This is how human beings are working. There is an infinite supply of thoughts and beliefs as well. Like your shopping. When you begin to tell yourself you are beautiful and it is practiced every day, the thought of ugliness washes away because you are constantly thinking you are so beautiful, you see.

Katherine (Weakly): All right.

Orion Council: Much has been said and we do appreciate this communication. You have a lot to think about, dear one. You are the intellectual one, we know you. Do not worry about creating new conscious beliefs. It is a lot of work and we are saying it is not necessary at all times, but you are wanting to establish a more heart-centered connection. So you must focus that energy on your heart. Do healing work with your heart. Which crystals work on your heart, and which colors and sounds work on your heart? Think of opening your heart chakra. You know of

106

the chakra systems, you know of energy — how it is transmitted, how it is focused in the physical world from the spirit world and so on. Focus on your heart and your love for God will be felt when your heart is open. What makes your heart sing? Think of songs to listen to that make you feel love in your heart. Think of the animals. Krista says so many are focusing on animals and we are saying those are one species, level of existence, that is focused on the pure heart-love. How do you feel when you are holding your cat? You feel love for your cat. You are feeling with your heart. You do not buy a cat because a cat will solve your problems. You have a cat because you love the cat. You LOVE your children! It's love, it's your heart — that's your heart. That is love that God feels for you at all times. Your heart is connected to the Earth. When you listen to sounds of the ocean you are feeling a love energy. Your heart is open. The fish — you love the fish. You are loving good music. You love instrumental sounds. You love certain instruments. Perhaps drums and trombones or trumpets or symbols or maracas or any other type of instrument. You have your favorite ones. You like symphonies, those are felt through the heart as well. You love eating certain foods; that is felt in the heart, as well. You love certain flowers and the colors of the flowers; that is in the heart, as well. You love certain animal sounds, when you listen to the birds, you are loving those sounds; that is felt in the heart, as well. Those animals are singing for you and telling you things. Are you listening to those animals? They are loving you and they are talking with you. Did you know that the plants are talking to you? They love you. Did you know that? Oh, your children love you immensely, but did you know that the grass loves you as well? That is your heart. Have you talked to the nature spirits, lately? They love you; that is in your heart. Even the beings you cannot see; they love you. Why would they come if they did not love you? Why, so many beings love you! So many are helping you love yourself. You must only see they are reflecting to you all the love you reflect out. It is coming back to you. You simply must allow for that love to come in, because you have put so much love out to others. Well, release that plate of energy from in front of your heart and allow it to come in. Accept that love that they are all shining back to you. All the love you have for ponies and unicorns — allow them to show that love back to you. Why not? Why do you think it is constantly giving? Healer, heal thyself. You are saying you are the healers, so why can't the healer be loved, when it is loved? Why do you place this plate of energy in front of your heart when you are loving all around you and all is loving you back? You must understand you are all part of the same energy flowing through.

Katherine: Is there a plate?

Orion Council: Perhaps. You may imagine in your mind that there is a silver plate in front of your heart chakra and that all in this room are wanting to pour love into your heart chakra to help you heal. Would you allow that to happen? Would you allow it?

Katherine: Move the plate?

Orion Council: Would you allow that to happen?

Katherine: Yes.

Orion Council: Please do that, now. See in your mind you are removing a plate, a metal plate that is in front of your heart chakra, about two feet from your body. Imagine that happening. Please take the plate with your right hand and put it on the floor. Now your heart chakra is open. There are many angelic beings in this room, pouring love into your heart chakra, right now. Please focus your energy on them, pouring this love into your heart chakra. Do you feel the energy, pouring into your heart chakra?

Katherine: Yes.

Orion Council: Good. Do you realize a unicorn next to you now?

Katherine: Hello.

Orion Council: Yes, you do not believe it but it is there. Unicorn saying that you must remember the unicorns. Seventh dimensional beings coming into this planet now, because so many have opened their hearts and want them to come in. So, they have allowed it to happen. Be proud of your fellow Creators on this planet, allowing for these energies to come in. It was not you alone who allowed this to happen. So many on your planet have asked the angels, "Please, angels, help my children. Help my neighbor. Help [President] Obama, and the other ones. Angels, come on in. Bring anyone you can to help heal this planet. I love my planet. Help my planet, please!" So they come. So they come, you see! Can you believe it? They come when you ask, the angels come in to your lives! Angels come in! We know you are troubled in believing it's happening, but we are telling you, it's happening.

Katherine: Why should I have trouble in believing that it's happening?

Orion Council: You do not see it; that's why. People have been taught to trust in what they see. In science classes, it is taught if it is not in the microscope, it does not exist. That is your belief and we are proving you incorrect. If you could see everything, you would be overwhelmed and you could not focus on this physical existence. If you could see everything that was around you, you would be confused and you could not focus on physicality, you see.

Katherine: There are those of us who have developed clairvoyance.

Orion Council: Yes, because they are here to help. That is their gift and they are living specific kinds of lives, you see. They are not the politicians, you see. Some will be able to see, but your mass consciousness is not ready for everyone to see because of the focus. You must release the old, first. You must release the warlike mentality. Before you see unicorns, you must release the old warlike mentality. Can you imagine if the psychic were focused on wars and on corruption and on injustice and on insurance and on controlling the masses? No, the psychic has a completely different set of intentions which is why they are seeing these etheric beings, you see.

If Obama were to see his unicorn, he would be so distracted he would fall over in his chair, and the White House would collapse, you see. But he still has a unicorn. Do you understand our point? If all were to see the angels, they would drop everything that was happening and the control would be released and someone else would possibly take over this control of your planet and you are not wanting that to happen. You are wanting the human beings to control your planet. One by one, these etheric beings are being ingrained in your society through people like yourselves, you see, which is why you are highly important, because it is needed. Just as cars are needed at this moment, so are the psychics, so are the healers, so are the artists and Creators of many other things. You all have roles to play and we are telling you, you are most important at this time because your role is to communicate the Divine to people. You realize you have potential to awaken others to spiritual concepts. You are doing quite well and your heart now has been allowing more love to flow in now because you consciously focused it, this way. We helped you with that. But you are the one who allowed it to happen. You know this yourself, you allowed the angel to pour in love energy to your heart chakra. Now, do you feel there is more love than yesterday? Perhaps you do.

Katherine: I say thank you to the angels, the unicorns, and to you, the Council, for your assistance. Thank you.

Orion Council: You are acting as if you are not ...Well, you have begun to realize your power. It will become more so in the future but you have done quite well. You are doing quite well.

Katherine: Thank you.

(Break)

Katherine: Krista, in your opinion, what's the difference between mediumship and channeling?

Krista: I think mediumship is giving proof of loved ones who have passed on.

Katherine: So what's the difference between giving proof of the deceased and channeling a deceased loved one?

Krista: I think it's the focus. Maybe mediumship focuses more on the astral plane because loved ones are coming in with their personalities. It's about human lives that have transitioned into Spirit and are connected to people in the audience. My mediumship classes taught me that there are rules: you identify the communicator, give evidence of how they died, their reason for coming and the message that they have. So it's a person who has had life experience on this planet. Channeling focuses more on different levels of existence. I'm channeling a group of entities who haven't had human lives. Okay, laughter signals…it tickles…okay.

Orion Council: Nice to talk with you. Yes, she is enjoying channeling now.

Katherine: How would you define channeling?

Orion Council: It is easy communication. It is when you talk to your Home, friends from Home. You are communicating with the other realms, not just one of the realms but many at the same time. You have to bring in energies from different levels. So, one is a mental level because you are using words and another is an etheric level because you are opening the channels and your energy system. You have activated many of these different layers of consciousness at the same time.

Katherine: That's what Krista is doing?

Orion Council: Yes, tapping into other layers of existence; other entrance ways to the soul…soul energy coming into the body. Yes, that is feeling nice. Krista is feeling nice about it. That is why she is laughs: it is her soul coming into her body, more. Yes.

Katherine: Is it accurate to say that this third dimension is toxic to the soul?

Orion Council: Not at all, it is only one experience for the soul. The soul has other places to focus its energy. "Toxic" is a human term, as is illusion — something humans do [along with] duality and separation. [The] soul is free to decide what to experience. Illusion is also part of the experience. That just is, it just is.

Katherine: When you all say things like, "you are so beautiful," what are you seeing?

Orion Council: We are seeing your energy, you know that.

Katherine: Energy signature?

Orion Council: Correct. It is a beautiful signature.

Katherine: Isn't every single energy signature in all of creation, beautiful?

Orion Council: Well, who lives in the dual system?

Katherine: We do.

Orion Council: Correct. So, there are those energies, not so beautiful to you.

Katherine: Well I'm asking your opinion, your perspective.

Orion Council: Ah, clever one; you are trying to trick a Spirit!

Katherine: Not trying to trick; just having a little fun, heh, heh.

Orion Council (Humorously): Well, you do a good job. We cannot say what we want to say now. You must hold onto your horses. It is not easy to describe this side.

Katherine: All right.

Orion Council: Many of us are wanting to tell you about the Other Side. It is not easy to describe.

Katherine: Please, share.

Orion Council: Okay. Many of us are wanting to tell you about the pretty things that are on this side of the veil. Are you wanting to know about those pretty things or something else?

Katherine: No, the "pretty things" would be wonderful. Thank you.

Orion Council: There are many unicorns in the room; the unicorns are coming through, again. They are hungry or something. They have energy for you to share with their planet. When you are talking with your unicorns they will give you a nudge of energy and will support your life mission. They want to give you energy to help you heal the land and set up a new paradigm for all.

Katherine: Can we speak with them now?

Orion Council: Can't quite. They have energy for you; want to tell you about the energies of their own kingdom but will be a different energy to transcribe. They are trying to say that you have to focus on the Earth, land. Land is important for your growth. You have gotten away from the land, they say. When you are on the land you feel the ancient wisdoms of the land. So, where are you going? That is an important thing because the land tells you what to focus on, too. Your focus changes in different landscapes. The unicorns are knowing that and they want you to go to these energy vortexes. Creation vortexes and other such ones of creating. Energy vortexes are their mission — helping create energy vortexes' power. They have to arrange people to create these energy vortexes. Are wanting people to discern between great places and not so great places for your energy centering itself. They are wanting you to help focus your light in these certain places. Many places for different people.

Katherine: What places?

(Interruption) Andromedan wants to help you with your question.

Katherine: Thank you. Welcome.

Andromedan: Hello, hello. Andromedan here, wanting to talk about your places of residence — the possibilities for residence. You can travel to many lands but you have to remember they are indeed focused energy vortexes and they will require that you assimilate to their energy centers and when you travel to these other places you will begin to bring in that energy of that place more, you see. You are light beacons, so when you go to these places, you will bring in more of the light of that place. Which kind of light are you wanting to bring in? You can bring in many different kinds of energies at this time, so it is about your focus and about what you are wanting. You can create many different avenues for love and light but you must remember to do that which your soul is wanting and you must connect with your soul first before you travel to these vortexes. You must see which one resonates with your energy and you must research them first. You cannot go blindly into these spaces without knowing the purpose of your travels. Sometimes, you will simply be drawn to these places because your soul is yearning to go to these places and thus will direct you, but you must also do the research on why you are going to these places. It will help you immensely in your life purpose. You will be able to teach other people about these places and so they will be able to be directed to these places as well.

Katherine: "Inner" research, or typical human research?

Andromedan: Typical human research we mean, of course. Typical human research.

Katherine: Any suggestions?

Andromedan: Yes, many in the South American continent for you, Katherine.

Katherine: Machu Picchu?

Andromedan: Well, of course. Good. You know it already.

Session 8

Katherine: I would like to start with a prayer: Kodoish, Kodoish, Kodoish, Adonai Tsebayoth.

Orion Council: Hello, friends. You are drawing us in quite quickly with the prayers.

Katherine: Oh, very good. Welcome.

Orion Council: Yes. How are you today?

Katherine: It's a rainy day and we're munching on delicious grapes.

Orion Council: Yes, you are enjoying the taste, yes. How wonderful to be physical.

Katherine: That's right.

Orion Council: Yes. What an amazing experience. You can witness textures and colors and emotions.

Katherine: And rainy days.

Orion Council: That is quite right.

Katherine: I have a quick question for you from Krista's online friend. What she wants to know is, if we are all ascending or will some be left behind.

Orion Council: Yes. Other channels [are] saying others will be left behind. Who is being left behind? What does that mean? How can Ascension occur if there are people not witnessing Ascension, or knowing about it? Other people are indeed in need of this curiosity that has been sparked

117

in lightworkers. Lightworkers are aware of the outer realms, the Other Side, so to speak, on the other side of the veil and what is going on. Lightworkers are constantly curious about those kinds of things. Those who are not aware of the workings of the Other Side are called "asleep." These people are simply not focused on this aspect of life, that you would call the Spirit World. Ascension is the focusing of energies. That is what the answer is. These people who are not ascending are not focusing on bringing in more of this communication with the Other Side. Ascension involves many things. Ascension involves a more benevolent outcome, a more benevolent behavior. Ascension is also incorporating more of the soul into the body. That is happening to all. Ascension also means indulging in this love that you are. It is a focusing of a newer love energy on this planet that has not been felt before. Those who do not realize this happening will be hit by a wave that they did not expect. They will live in fear, so to speak. That is why they would be needing the lightworkers to explain to them what had just happened. "Why do I not quarrel? I was taught to quarrel with the other one when they showed me their horrible side. I was taught to quarrel with them, why do I not quarrel with them?" They wonder about these things. Lightworkers may not speak of Spirit but they will have that benevolent behavior ingrained. They understand why they are behaving benevolently and explain to others why these things are happening. Others will be knocked over with shock sometimes at what happens. It is like not being prepared for a race. Time is speeding up so to speak, time is changing its dimensional focus, not the same as before. How do you explain this to others who are not even aware of a Spirit World? Many are also wondering why people are concerned about the Spirit World when they live in the physical. They are "asleep" so to speak because they do not question these things. Curiosity is what separates these people. When the lightworker begins to understand more of who he or she is, the lightworker is able to bring in the new paradigm of behavior and living; change-makers, so to speak. Those who are not aware of what is going on will be in the midst of change without the right vehicles, you see. How to drive when the road has completely changed? They will simply follow the road. The masses will be following that road that the lightworkers have created for them. Lightworkers are building new roads and the old ones are crumbling down. They will have to turn onto the correct road, if they want to cross the bridge, you see. They have options as well. They do not have to cross that bridge I if they do not want to but change is inevitable—even your sociologists say that change is constant. So if you consider a crumbling bridge while a new bridge is being built, how does it make you feel? Afraid, or positively focused on the new bridge? Some see it as falling off a bridge: "how terrible, how horrible to fall into the water," while others will rejoice at the fact of becoming one with the ocean again. Remember, you are a wave of the ocean. It is all a choice but change is inevitable.

Katherine: Is it a question of gradual changes or immediate Earth changes or will each individual's experience depend on how they are focused?

Orion Council: Earth changes can be manipulated by the inhabitants of Earth as long as they are focusing on the Earth, you see, which is why benevolent outcomes are wonderful tools because many are able to focus on "benevolent" hurricanes, you see. Earth changes will happen as they always do, but a human being can affect, just as a prayer can affect when it is a pure intention.

Katherine: Sometimes I have felt that I had an effect on the weather when I asked for the rains to come only after I have gotten inside.

Orion Council: Well, you are witnessing your personal mastery and power. Many human beings are afraid of shifts and shifts have always happened. In your life, you have moved to new homes. You are, as a species, quite well equipped for change to happen. It is always fear that comes into play when you are asked to move out of a comfortable place. You creatures of habit want to stay in your habit zones although you intellectually understand that that the change will serve you immensely because your soul will experience immense growth and prosperity from the change. Still, people stay in the same homes and holes because they do not want to leave their comfort zones.

Session 9

(Editor's note: Katherine strikes Angel Tuning Forks.)

Krista: I'm having a good time on Earth right now, that's all I've got to say!

Katherine: Okay, let's pray: Kodoish, Kodoish, Kodoish Adonai Tsebayoth.

Orion Council: Well done. Well done. We are ready to communicate with you.

Katherine: Welcome.

Orion Council: Hello. How can we help you this evening? We are wanting to discuss Ascension with you.

Katherine: Yes! We are ready.

Orion Council: We are ready as well to begin the text of Ascension. Yes, many topics we can discuss with your text. Yes, your text can cover a range of topics about Ascension and how it is affecting everyone on the planet.

Katherine: Is there a way of preparing for Ascension?

Orion Council: Well, you can focus on the light within of course, but that is our obvious response. You can also focus light within other people but that is also is an obvious response. You can focus on the light within the nature but that, of course, is an obvious response. We are saying this because we want you to do this constantly throughout your daily lives. You are wanting Ascension badly now and we are saying that this will bring it about even in a faster manner than before. So how many people will attune to this light within? That is the question now. You are all wanting to speed up things in your experience to the better future, so we are saying more light, more light, more light. That is what we are saying. You can also focus the light within other planets as well outside of your solar system. It will help All-That-Is, you see – also a task of lightworkers – so many options. Can channel information of other places as well; wisdoms from other places –so many options. You are all identifying with the core beliefs you hold. Many of you are ready and preparing to release old core beliefs. You have held on to many core beliefs for too long. Many are not quite in your best interest at this time: old beliefs about feeling unimportant—not a good belief to hold in your energy field. Not feeling good enough or not loving yourself or others, not appreciating them and their efforts [are] all core beliefs. Forget about them, we say. Now you are releasing those beliefs. Bit by bit you are coming to terms with who-you-really-are.

Katherine: Who are you referring to now?

Orion Council: We are discussing humanity. Now as humanity comes to terms with who they are, they will begin this new energy figure [configuration] of light coming in. Sacred geometries are coming in now. Scientists will work with these energies. They will begin to implement these new structures on a quantum level. A new dimension is coming into being.

Katherine: Such as tetrahedrons, that sort of thing?

Orion Council: Yes, of course, these are ones of many geometries. The new Ascension begins later on, you see. You are ascending; it happens in stages. New stage will happen in quite a short time.

Katherine: November 11, 2011, for example?

Orion Council: Yes, so close to beginning of November: new period of beginning, awakening more people, you see. This is why it is a great opportunity for us to discuss with you opportunities to help others. Others will be looking to you for help. You have the opportunity to focus the light within others. You are doing good job, we say more to do. You have to remember you can accomplish anything you want. Many are wanting our advice, it is all right but you are the ones with the life experience, you are the one living on Earth. Better you tell them how to heal themselves. Better you be the instructor. They are wanting instructions on how to live – you humans like instructions, it is so easy to have them: don't need to create.

Katherine: Well, we should be about creating, shouldn't we?

Orion Council: Yes, of course. Always experimenting, of course you want stability: also habit of humans. You want everyone to agree, as well, with your concepts. It's hard to be a unique one when you are feeling alone. Do not worry because you are keen on creating constantly. You will never be alone, you are important part of All-That-Is. You have to remember to focus the light within yourself is to appreciate God. Those who do not, will be summoned to do so. Others are noticing their attention spans are not so long as before. They are wanting new experiences so they cannot hold on to the past ones. It's letting-go-time now. Anytime you remember the past it is not as clear as it once was. That's okay, you are not losing your memories. They are still existing, they are simply not in your waking state of mind. When you are a creative wave of thought, you are not remembering, you are using the past to make the future. You are appreciating something in your past to create because it is a positive creation. Are you understanding our talk tonight?

Katherine: Yes, except for that last piece. You said that we use the past to create our future?

Orion Council: Using the past to create the future but not remembering unhappy moments.

Katherine: But we could do it differently? We do not have to create from the past which is what we already know – isn't that so?

Orion Council: Using past *understandings* to create the future.

Katherine: Ah, now I understand, past understandings, thank you.

Orion Council: Yes, okay. How are you?

Katherine: I am fine. You are a different energy.

Orion Council: Yes, Keeper [Krista] says we sound Jamaican.

Katherine: Well, not quite.

Orion Council: You are thinking we sound Jamaican?

Katherine (Laughing): Well, I don't but —

Orion Council: Okay, Krista thinking that we are Jamaican Orion.

(Laughter)

Orion Council: We are Orion Council.

Katherine: But yours is a different energy signature.

Orion Council: Yes! You understand.

Katherine: So maybe we will call you, "The Jamaican."

Orion Council: Yeah, not quite but you can do that.

(Laughter)

Orion Council: It's okay. We are happy here all the time.

Katherine: Are you eight here right now?

Orion Council: Eight. Yes.

Katherine: When you say, "not all of us are here," where do the others go?

Orion Council: Focusing otherwise; not focused on this room.

Katherine: So one might be focused on another channel, for instance?

Orion Council: Okay, now you get tricky question for us: how do we focus our energies? Many of us have to try to focus it one time but we can also undo that energy if we want to undo it. We can train you to do this as well but it's not easy. You would be focusing your entire body, for example, at one time; it's hard to do. When you try to focus your energy on all your muscles, Krista says, you cannot. It's good metaphor, yes? You can try but it's hard. You are relaxing energy, you are not vibrating so rapidly in that space—conserving perhaps, not exactly, like trying to forgive the –hold on. You can try to understand us. We are saying it's like one of us tries to attune to the room energy and another attunes to the frequency of the vibration. One of us attunes to the verbal communication, to the language of you, and other one to the energies in the room: focusing on the room space, how this room is using its energy, how you are attuning to the energy in the room.

Katherine: Can you elaborate on the energy in the room right now?

Orion Council: Yes, we add to the room, we add energies to the room.

Katherine: Aren't there always energies present in this room?

Orion Council: Of course but it's a focusing. It is existing but not focusing here.

Katherine: I have another question for you.

Orion Council: Yes?

Katherine: I once read that quanta, little "energy packets," sort of flash in and out, depending on where our focus is. If I focus on, "I am going to my house," the quanta create the house, so I feel that I am going into my house. When I leave my house and I'm no longer thinking about it, the quanta "flash out," so to speak and the house is "gone." Is that how it works?

Orion Council: The house can exist in other dimensions as well, it is not only one dimension. You can leave your house behind in other dimensions, you see. You can create a house and come back later, that's just like in the physical world but when you leave you are just creating a new path. If you have walked that path, it is still there, it does not disappear. The thought form exists. That is how it is created, you see. In your physical world you have many layers of being. You cannot see most layers. In this physical realm you have tiny atoms, yes? You have tiny, tiny particles. You are just not focusing on these tiny particles but they are still there. All that makes up the physical world has its own aspects as well. You have the ability to choose between which aspects you want to focus on. Do you focus on the way you cut the table into layers or do you focus on the cells of the pieces of wood? You can chop up the table into many slivers of wood. It is a question of, well, is there a table anymore? It is a different form. You are discussing how the form simply changes because the energy is not changing. The form is still existing but you are rearranging the pieces of the table. What was once a house became a road. The thought form is still existing but you used the house to create the road. You are reusing energy. It does not disappear, you just cannot focus on it constantly that is why you think it turns off and on.

Katherine: So that is not accurate?

Orion Council: It turns off to *your* perception. It is still there but your focus is on another layer of existence.

Katherine: So it seems that everything goes back to what we focus on.

Orion Council: Of course!

Katherine: So, if we put out our hand and focused on

making an apple appear, would it appear, if we believed it?

Orion Council: Yes, however it would take more time for you. It would take more time for it to appear, for you.

Katherine: Is it the same for healing? When there is something hurting or some problem in the body, is it a question of focusing on it as being whole, complete and healthy and therefore we create that in ourselves?

Orion Council: Yes, however you need to have the template for a healthy body first to create the health. You must have it prepared. This seems to contradict the creating [process] but when you have this new template with the one already in existence, you will be able to fit the form into the thought. So you must have the template.

Katherine: And the template is within the mind?

Orion Council: It is like the opposite in a photograph; you have the opposite color of the image. It is like a cast that you are going to fill first.

Katherine: And once we have that template, we must hold onto it, not contradict it with opposing thoughts, changing the mind?

Orion Council: Yes, you must hold your focus, of course.

Katherine: Is it accurate to say that as human beings we hop from one thing to another? We tend to focus a little bit here and then hop to another thought over there, then hop quickly to another and that is why we −

Orion Council: You are conditioned to "hop around." That

is your conditioning. All human beings have opportunities to change that conditioning but they do not because they enjoy the stimulation, enjoy feeling that there is always something new. You are distracted but you enjoy the distraction. You can learn to focus if you want to.

Katherine: Is that where meditation comes in, for example?

Orion Council: Yes, people meditate for answers.

Katherine: Kodoish, Kodoish, Kodoish Adonai Tsebayoth.

Orion Council: We are here, yes. Hello, friends. We are wanting to discuss Ascension with you. You are all not focusing the light within yourselves. You must remember, "She is doing that, she is looking at herself as if she were light.'" That is requested. Imagine you are made of light. Constantly imagine you and others are made of light. Use your inner eyesight. Seeing all as light as the snow, however on the inside. You are light. Remember that.

Katherine: I'm a little surprised that you say we are not focusing.

Orion Council: You are focusing on mundane things. You are focusing on your everyday activities, you are not focusing on the light that you are.

Katherine: So that means more meditation?

Orion Council: More of this meditation, yes. We are knowing that you are all busy people but remember to do this at times, during the day. It is most important to focus the light within yourselves.

Katherine: Thinking and feeling — that's the focusing, right?

Orion Council: When you are imagining you are light, how do you feel? You are light. How does it feel? How does it feel? How does it feel? Is it feeling heavy? A burden?

Katherine: No, light and airy.

Orion Council: You like that feeling. It is good for you.

Katherine: I'm doing it now.

Orion Council: Yes.

Katherine: Can you tell?

Orion Council: We are knowing your vibrations. You have one of focused energy on this part of you that wants to be expressed. You are noticing those aspects now wanting to be expressed. You are discussing them with your friends. You are wanting to express a new part of yourself that has not been expressed before. It is a part of the Ascension.

Katherine: But are these mundane areas?

Orion Council: They are not mundane. You are focusing on mundane sometimes when you are not focused on the light. You are focusing on, "where do I put my cup" and "when do I close the door, how do I close the window." You are not focusing on the light when you do that. More focusing on the light.

Katherine: Isn't [reciting] Kuthumi's Prayer, focusing the light?

Orion Council: Your prayer works to a certain extent. You must believe it works.

Katherine: But my question is, isn't that an example of focusing the light?

Orion Council: Yes.

Katherine: Even using affirmations, isn't that a way of focusing the light throughout the day?

Orion Council: It is a focus on what you are wanting to become. Affirmations are what you want to become mostly. More assured, or feeling more safe, or wanting more positive expectation —that is affirmation.

Katherine: Well, what of the statement "I AM LIGHT" as an affirmation?

Orion Council: It is a truth. You are remembering but you must feel it, too.

Katherine: What are some ways to remember who we are?

Orion Council: To remember who you are, is to understand that you are eternal. It is an entry into a space where you know you can become anything you want. It is an expansive state of being. Expansion is necessary to become: you become expansion, you see. You, becoming expansion, is your true Self. You are expanding, always expanding.

Katherine: What are some techniques, tips, or methods that will be helpful to remember who we are?

Orion Council: You can have photos of light—more. There are not enough photos in your home of Light Beings. You can have angel pictures: many that symbolize your light. As we discussed previously, your symbols are important to you humans. You want symbols because they have meaning and energy in them. When someone creates artwork and says it is healing artwork, you feel that energy, you see. It's as if you held an object and you knew who had that object. You understand? You know a vibration of a house because someone else lived in the house. You can change it, but it is still reminding you — like the artwork. You can have more artwork in your life. Not enough artwork. You need to remember who you are at all times, you see. This is why we say artwork is most important at this time, for all need more artwork, more artwork.

Katherine: Our book could include artwork.

Orion Council: Yes, but you also need images because people are visual people. You can have sounds as well that make you feel at home, a sound, CD, what is home music like? What is Divine music to you? More images of what Divine is, then you will feel that vibration when you look at that picture.

Katherine: All right, that is something very concrete that we can do, thank you.

Orion Council: You are welcome, friend. You are our friend, we love you.

Katherine: And we love you.

Orion Council (Joking): Of course, we are amazing.

Katherine: Yes, quite! May I ask a few more questions?

Orion Council: No more time, good bye. Joking.

Katherine (Laughing): The new grid: could you please comment on the new grid that has formed?

Orion Council: There are many parts — axes — that have been finished. Many anchored in this new realm. There are anchored parts in this world. There are many anchors of light, anchoring the light in the new grid, the beautiful grid. It's a beautiful grid, you see: all around this Earth. It's so beautiful, so many anchored light beams. So many pillars. Krista says she will draw you a picture, it's like a dome with many pillars. It's a beautiful axis of Earth. Axis of Earth is shifting. Many now [are] attuning to this new grid — attuning to the energies. You are feeling it. It is a positive vibration coming in. Oh, your children are feeling it; your husband is feeling it; the animals know it. You are knowing it, too. It's here, already. It's prepared, quite finished, almost. It's got many pillars anchoring itself onto this planet. The change will be a beautiful one when everyone steps into this new grid. You will see a change on the planet, it is a beautiful change.

Katherine: Is the change imminent or are we talking 20 years from now?

Orion Council: No, it is here, but many need to attune first. Many need to. [It's] not a part of the Earth yet. It's coming, it's coming. It's here but it's not anchored in the Earth, yet.

Katherine: Is the attunement an ongoing or a gradual process?

Orion Council: It needs to be placed on the surface; it is not on the surface of Earth, yet. There are pillars connecting from the Earth to the grid. These are in those special places that you know. These special places are anchoring these pillars.

Katherine: Oh, the sacred sites.

Orion Council: Yes. A portal here, a portal there, helping to anchor the grid. It's been cast, it's just wanting to settle.

It takes years to settle. It takes years to settle onto the Earth, but many new pillars [are] bringing it closer to the Earth's surface.

Katherine: Wonderful, thank you. I will ask Krista to draw a picture later. She was feeling very drained on the computer today.

Orion Council: Yes, she is focusing too much on others' problems now, helping them. Stop helping everyone, Krista. She's focusing on her friends to help them, always helping. Stop it.

Katherine: Well, what do you suggest she do instead?

Orion Council: Need time to relax into her own space. At times she remembers and at times she forgets because she needs to help someone. Always helping is not good. Stop it.

Katherine: All right. I'm sure she heard that.

Orion Council: You too, Katherine. Now you'll have to focus on what you want. Be the example to your children of being a "good selfish." Necessary. You'll show them. They will understand. You understand?

Katherine: Yes.

Orion Council: You're a good mom. Oh, so good mom! Golden Mom. Enough is expressed to the other ones. You need to focus on what you want, now. Too much expression with others. Too much expression with others. Need to focus on yourself. Are you listening? Please.

Katherine: I hear you, I'm taking it in. Thank you.

(Break)

Orion Council: Can we continue?

Katherine: Yes, please do.

Orion Council: That you are awake to these new energies — you will realize you are changing in your perceptions of others. You are changing what you are wanting to express with other people as well. No longer these old patterns, they are not necessary anymore, you see. New changes. New changes happening and new parts of you are wanting expression.

Katherine: New aspects?

Orion Council: Well, aspects have been with you but they are new to you.

Katherine: So, is it becoming <u>aware</u> of the aspects, then?

Orion Council: You know yourself, they are shouting almost. You will find affinities to new aspects, new parts of life. An affinity to certain things, you will have and you will see what you are becoming.

Katherine: Is it possible to release some of the old aspects that are no longer of interest?

Orion Council: No need to release anything, you simply are like a snowball moving down the mountain, you see. Do not worry.

Katherine: You were saying before, that Krista needs to ask for help, for example, to ask her best friends and the last thing that you pointed out was to ask them about choices. What did you mean by that?

Orion Council: They can provide perspectives on different choices [like] where to live and good things about different places on this Earth.

Katherine: Why does she need to ask others for that?

Orion Council: Not necessary but helpful to gain a perspective on what places are like. It will serve a purpose, you see. It does not mean they will influence her. They may influence her to do otherwise. They say "go here," she says "no," you see. Depends on the person who is speaking. Very interesting, what happens. Sometimes you need an enemy to become your best friend to show you what to change.

Katherine: Okay. Another question?

Orion Council: Yes, of course.

Katherine: Simultaneous time, simultaneous existence, this illusion of time that we humans have as linear, could you comment on this? Perhaps you would have a better term than simultaneous time for everything happening in the now?

Orion Council: Time is one-dimensional. You are living in five dimensions. How can a 5-dimensional being live in one dimension? It's hard to become so simple when you are so complex. When you look at time, it is to structure your focus. When you focus on time you feel a sense of continuity. You feel a sense of "worthwhile." You see your progress. This is why this dimension is added because a human being needs to feel they have accomplished, completed something, when in fact, nothing is complete. You want this experience because you see how when you focus on one thing at a time, you can grow in many different ways. From the densest part of reality, you can make something grow into something quite large. It is like planting a seed. So many of you are wanting to see proof of your fifth dimensional existence. It is there, but time itself has not caught up with your fifth dimensional selves.

Session 11

Orion Council: Many are not knowing who they are.

Katherine: Most of us, but many are endeavoring to remember. You said something about people reflecting back to us so, this woman, saying she is an archangel and my feeling of skepticism, or resistance, is what? Can you help me understand?

Orion Council: You are not enjoying the fact that someone can claim such a thing. You have programmed yourself not to believe in such "nonsense." It is "nonsense."

Katherine: I think, I feel, like it's ego but you are telling me that is incorrect. Is that accurate?

Orion Council: What is ego's position [role]? To explain reality to you, perhaps?

Katherine: No.

Orion Council: Ego wants to tell you how it is, so, when you have a contradictory message, you will not accept it. You have a filter for the "B.S." You will think that these things are not real, but if you can talk to Orion, can she be an angel?

Katherine: I suppose so.

Orion Council: If you can talk to Orion, can she be an angel?

Katherine: This "B.S." filter —

Orion Council: Well, we use a human term for not believing all that you are told.

Katherine: Yes, but, when we say "B.S." filter, it's very specific. We feel that it —

Orion Council: You are not enjoying our response.

Katherine: I am not totally understanding. You told us she is an angel, so that's it.

Orion Council: You are not liking the fact that the one who is an angel claims they are. Such a person should be quiet, should they not?

Katherine: I know, that's my belief.

Orion Council: They should not share such things. Others would not like it. Do not tell others you are an angel. They will not like you.

Katherine: Instead show it. I would say, demonstrate it!

Orion Council: Why not say it with your words? You liked our singing, did you not?

Katherine: Yes.

Orion Council: Well, it is one way of expression, dear one, one way to express yourself. All is a creative process, friend. Some do not know how to speak at all. Some creatures on this planet cannot speak. When they have the ability a fox would say, "I am a fox!" If they had a voice all of a sudden, "I am a fox," it would say. What about the angel, having a voice?

Katherine: I see your point.

Orion Council: Difficult lesson, dear friend, to accept one another is not easy, especially when they are seeming to be liars.

Katherine (Laughing): Well, I think I am a little closer to accepting the angel part. But to say that she is an archangel is, for me, over the top.

Orion Council: Well, we will advise her not to say such things because this is, well, a taboo in your society. An archangel is amazing energy. One human could not hold this energy without transcending the body.

Katherine: Exactly.

Orion Council: Our friend Krista wants to know as well. We will answer you. This friend was wanting to hear specific words. She heard what she wanted to hear. All is well. Just another one talking, just one person, talking. Perhaps you want to know and want to discern between the right and the wrong, friend. You are wanting to say, "This was correct of her, but this was incorrect of her." You can decide that, too. It is not always to your benefit to become involved in such matters however you are an interesting one. You are wanting to discover the egotistical aspects and to eliminate them.

Katherine: Yes.

Orion Council: Quite a human way to behave: find the darkness and turn it away. First find the darkness and tell it to leave.

Katherine: How about shine the light?

Orion Council: Well, what about *that*? Now you are tapping into who-you-are, dear one. You are all love, you see.

Katherine: Yes, but there is a difference, isn't there, between being judgmental and being discerning? I don't want to be judgmental, I do want to discern.

Orion Council: When you speak aloud your judgment or discernment, you amplify the energy of that action. Just as our friend amplified that she is an angel, that is her focus. You can focus that you were correct: "That day, on the November evening, I was correct about one woman, I knew her right and I knew her wrong. That was that night." Do you feel better, friend? Perhaps not. We were joking with you. Perhaps not feeling so good after a judgment. Discerning to protect you, yes, to show you how to become a more allowing Creator. Yes, use it as an avenue, like gears, to switch the gears, you will find the right path. Must shift gears. Use it as a way to go in the direction you are wanting to go in.

Katherine: Part of my feeling is that I want to protect Krista, too.

Orion Council: No need, but you are helping. No need to protect a Creator.

Katherine: True.

Orion Council: You are finished with your questions?

Katherine: I'm still not clear precisely. Am I sitting in judgment of this person?

Orion Council (Dryly): Is there a correct answer? What is right and wrong? How biblical.

Katherine: Not right or wrong but which is wiser, a more understanding, a gentler approach?

Orion Council: Which one feels like graciousness? To feel that she is needy or to feel that she deserves self-love?

Katherine: She, of course, deserves self-love.

Orion Council: She needed to hear those words. Imagine if your well-being depended on some words you wanted to hear. Imagine. You would feel compassion towards her?

Katherine: Yes.

Orion Council: Yes, that is a lesson.

Katherine: Thank you. *Thank you.* I got it.

Orion Council: Well done. We are quite finished. We enjoy our discussion with you.

Katherine: Thank you and goodnight.

Krista: That was a good one.

Katherine: That was a good one — another good one. It's such a different feeling to feel compassion rather than to sit in judgment.

Session 12

Krista: Wednesday, November 2, 2011.

Katherine: 11-2-11

Krista: 11, 2, 2, 11. I saw a lot of 1's and 2's on the clock. I've seen a lot of things, lately.

Orion Council: Council is here wanting to discuss Ascension.

Katherine: Welcome.

Orion Council: Hello, friend. We are glad to have this conversation with you. Yes, Ascension is a program. Krista wanted validation. It is a program. It is a set-up for the Ascension of the Planet Earth. It was a set-up for all to awaken. Now everyone is awakening, slowly. Some are, slowly awakening. Do not worry. Slowly, they will awaken. It is happening now.

Katherine: It sounds as if Ascension is a process, an on-going sort of process, not an event. Is that correct?

Orion Council: Yes, it is a process of creating a heaven on Earth, as you said: Heaven on Earth. Well, how does it feel to be in heaven? Ha, ha, ha. What are you wanting to experience, friend?

Katherine: Well, "Heaven on Earth" sums it up very nicely.

Orion Council: You are wondering what it means to Ascend. It is a process of creating a heaven on Earth. What else is it? It is a gathering of like-minded individuals on the planet, as all help. Communities will change, you see: like-minded people, finding each other, now; all traveling to other places. Like-minded people are meeting each other; happening now, too. Do not worry. Communities developing, yes, communities gathering together for the new reign of this new history.

Katherine: Will Krista and I find these communities and be a part of them?

Orion Council: Well, you will be creating them quite soon. You will create these communities soon.

Katherine: When you say soon what do you mean? We have a certain —

Orion Council: Well, it is not something your eyes can see, but, you are contributing to many communities in your daily tasks.

Katherine: Okay. That's good to know.

Orion Council: Yes, you will ascend as well. You will ascend as well. These new communities are Ascended people; Ascended people. These are people, who are awake to us, for example. One community, many others existing soon: communities of the energy. You participate in one, "I Am Light" yes?

Katherine: Yes.

Orion Council: Yes. You have a community. Small, but will become a community. It is eventually happening in that location, yes. There will be a community there and in many other places. Smaller, but not as small as your community in the I Am Light location. Other places will have these communities.

Katherine: Where?

Orion Council: Interesting. The equator, the area of the equator. The communities close to the equator. You will see changes happening, starting there.

Katherine: When you say the equator, you mean, all around the world?

Orion Council: Yes, all around the world.

Katherine: What of those who are still not awake — the people with whom we are very close who are not awake yet?

Orion Council: Yes. They will have to awaken. They will have to.

Katherine: But, if we are talking about Ascending —

Orion Council: They will feel uncomfortable if they do not focus on the love that they are. They will feel uncomfortable as before, however now, much more so. Things will not simply be allowed anymore. Energy will not allow for confusion and mistrust, and other such options. No, no more of those things. We are wanting to discuss Ascension.

Katherine: Yes. I am wondering if those people will be left behind? Will we be separated from them in some way?

Orion Council: Well, some will be left behind to realize what they have done. They will have to realize what they have done.

Katherine: So they have to become aware?

Orion Council: Yes. They have to know what is happening. They will be shown what is happening. If they cannot Ascend, they will have to leave.

Katherine: Leave the planet?

Orion Council: Yes.

Katherine: I see, I see.

Orion Council: Do not worry, friend. Do not worry.

Katherine: Yes. There is no death.

Orion Council: Some are awake; they simply do not want to discuss it. Many are Ascending. They do not know and are not consciously aware, however their patterns suit the new energy, you see. They have practiced already such a benevolent way of living, you see. No need to change their perceptions. Simply accept that they also are ascending. No need to discuss with everyone. New energies are in. You have witnessed them, already. There are many new beings on the Earth. New beings, new beings.

Katherine: In what form?

Orion Council: Nice question. Wait a moment. Some are these, friendly aliens. Friendly aliens.

Katherine: And their form? Are they human form, or are they —

Orion Council: Are fine energy, fine.

Katherine: Oh, fine energy. Etheric?

Orion Council: Yes. Angels want to experience Ascension, as well.

Katherine: How do they experience it?

Orion Council: They attune to a human life. They want to help with Ascension. They cannot choose what they want, no. Want to assist humans.

Katherine: And that is how they ascend? By assisting humans?

Orion Council: They will ascend. Yes.

Katherine: And the friendly aliens that are in etheric form — how do they ascend?

Orion Council: With the knowledge they gain about Earth. They are studying, yes, but they are knowing about Earth.

Katherine: Krista spoke today, about feeling new energy and feeling different things.

Orion Council: Yes, the new energy creates Oneness Consciousness. Oneness is a new way of life.

Katherine: When Krista and I were talking earlier about new forms of relationships, she made a comment about new ways of interacting, new ways of relating between men and women, between humans.

Orion Council: Yes, the new energy will not allow for control of the other one. It will be a mutual assistance of the other one. A love of the other one, to want to the best for them, will be more compatible in the new energy. People will become more sensitive to the new duration of a new life. A new lifetime will attune the energies. New people will become One with the Oneness Life. You will see a new life with Oneness energy.

Katherine: Wonderful! That's worth waiting for.

Orion Council: Yes. We are wanting to discuss Ascension. To agree with the Ascension process is helpful to us.

Katherine: How do we go about "agreeing" with the Ascension Process?

Orion Council: Believe it is true. To believe in it, will create it. Pretty much, when you agree with it, you will create it. Agree it is happening. Yes, you want it to happen. We know your energy. Do not worry. No one is bad. No one is bad. Everyone wants the best for everyone, truly.

Session 13

Krista: This is a "beginning month" because everything is eleven-something-eleven.

Katherine: Yes, lovely.

Krista: So every day is bringing in a new energy, this month, I think.

Katherine: I feel that way when I write it.

Orion Council: Hello, friends. How are you?

Katherine: Wonderful, how are you?

Orion Council: We are fine. We are wanting to discuss Ascension, of course.

Katherine: Of course.

Orion Council: How is it that you are ascending? Well, many human beings at this time are ascending. At this moment, they are ascending, remembering who they are. It was a process. You have seen it unfold. You have seen people remembering their own power. For example, manifestation power is one example of how to remember who you are. It is a skill that you have: an innate capability to manifest that which you want. You have will, with that you manifest. Yes? Questions today, yes? We are ready.

Katherine: Krista had a question about the dream state and the astral.

Orion Council: She has been juggling in the astral plane. She has been visiting her friends. She cares about her friends and she visits them to help them with their own Ascension. They have to ascend as well.

Katherine: In addition to hints from the future, I would like to know about the dynamics of Ascension, the process of Ascension. That suggests more than just potential futures, right?

Orion Council: You are wanting a template to create upon. You are wanting to focus your energies on the things that bring you joy, so this is why we would discuss these joyful topics because the humans are wanting to create them. A book about the possibilities will make people focus on the positive future. Positive future, most important.

Katherine: Okay! Now, we're *cookin' with gas.*

Orion Council (Bursts out laughing): Yes! You are cooking! Ha, ha, ha, ha! You are cooking!

Katherine (Laughing also): You like that one?

Orion Council (Laughing): You are cooking, yes. Ha, ha, hah! We are enjoying your humor. Yes, we are cooking, yes. We are cooking a lot of things. Creating, yes. We are creating with the fire energy, yes. Ha, ha! Very funny, you are. Angels are liking you. Ha, ha, ha!

Katherine: This is a wonderful thing that you're saying. People want joyful topics and this will help to bring more joy, more light in. Now, that is most wonderful.

Orion Council: A book of light. A book of light, in the home, in the office, in the room, yes.

Katherine: That will be quite stunning. You mentioned a template and I would like to develop a template for this book.

Orion Council: We meant a template for the future but you can also have one for the book. Many are wanting to know about the channeling process. What is happening? Perhaps a chapter regarding the channeling process; what it is, [is] most important for those who want to channel. And of course, that will change the future. How about more channels, instead of the psychics?

Katherine: Can you distinguish between psychics and channels, please?

Orion Council: Yes, a psychic is listening to the other energy and channeling is speaking the other energy. Psychic listens. Channel speaks. The psychic is seeing and listening, but is not really explaining as the Spirit would. Psychic is explaining in human terms. Of course, a channel does as well, but it is a somewhat different energy perspective. So many psychics, now. Need more channels. How about everyone a channel. How about that?

Katherine: Well, is it necessary to have another person asking the questions, or can someone sort of self-channel, [through automatic writing] like Krista did before?

Orion Council: Yes, they can do this, yes. They just simply do not trust in the process. They do not trust that they can do this.

Katherine: Is there a certain element of fear, not knowing what is coming through, or who is coming through them?

Orion Council: Yes, there are many rules, there are many lessons to learn with the channeling, yes. Self-respect is a big one.

Katherine: Can you explain a little more fully what you mean by that?

Orion Council: A channel must have self-respect, a channel must have self-respect.

Katherine: A sort of integrity?

Orion Council: Yes, a channel must feel that they deserve this communication and they also must feel that they are needing this and that others need this and so on. They must be in a state of service. In order to channel for others, they must be in a state of service. Channel does not want to trick another one. Channel must also appreciate spirituality, so to speak. Have a regard, an experience with occultic traditions, must realize they are trying to bring in the new way of life. They will understand they are going to help the Ascension process and they have beliefs such as these that will help them with the channeling and so they can do it easily because they do not have such problems as what is truth and what is not, what is a lie and what is not in alignment. They are able to discern between the energies.

Katherine: Are channels, then, in a sense, selected by Spirit?

Orion Council: Not as you would think, not as you would think. No, not as if it is a competition, not at all. No, no, no, no, no, no, no, no, no. You see, many can channel but they have to have a set of beliefs available to them. They must have a set of beliefs. Do not worry, many have their own gifts, you see.

Katherine: Yes, yes, everyone has their own gifts. I was just thinking about your question of everyone channeling or more people channeling.

Orion Council: Yes. So what if everyone created artwork? What if everyone were painting, or something? Different kinds of channels and different kinds of paintings: everyone can paint, you see.

Katherine: Yes, but you mentioned before about the fear aspect. Is it, in a sense, a legitimate fear that there may be entities that are —

Orion Council: Yes, yes, of course. It is up to the intention of the channel. This you must remember: what is the intention? To create more light, or to play games? What is the intention? All options are open. Good questions. We are enjoying your questions very much.

Katherine: Well, I'm enjoying you answers very much. All right. Joyful topics.

Orion Council: What are you enjoying in your own life? Shopping, perhaps? We can help with that, too, but we do not think it is necessary for the book. Joking, however. Many of you are not remembering the importance of the physical reality. Dear ones, you came to experience physicality at its finest. You must remember how much joy you feel when you are physical. Many of you are not remembering how you wanted to hold hands with your friends. You discussed with Krista how wonderful to hold the hands of the ones loved, yes? You enjoy being physical. It is an expression of God, yes. Little animals and pets and so on, furnitures and textures and substances; the effects of eating certain substances: some, you feel energized, some you feel relaxed. Interesting, to have these options in the physical reality. We believe that the channeling aspect is important in this world because everyone must realize that in order to remember who they are, they must realize their opportunities and so if everyone were to channel they would realize they had spiritual guidance at all times available to them. They simply need to experience channeling because they simply do not believe, however they will begin [to] slowly. Many do not need channeling to believe, however many [others] are wanting to experience that.

Katherine: So, as far as the book is concerned, it would be important to have chapters on what we might call "better humanhood" or enjoying this human experience.

Orion Council: Yes. You [can] discuss romantic relationships. It is one way of enjoying your human experience. Romantic relationships, are very much enjoyable. What else do you like? You enjoy decorating and you enjoy colors and you enjoy artwork and music. How important these all are. In the new world they will become more important. Sharing ideas, "very psychic," Krista says, "artwork is very psychic." Yes, it is opening the psychic channels when you are creating artwork. It is translating ideas, creation is happening at all levels, you see. You believe as a physical person you are not creating; this is a belief of many. They are thinking that God rules all. This is true but everything is creating more unto itself and so on and so forth. You must understand that to create is what brings you joy, you see. Are you creating a beautiful home? Are you creating a beautiful clothing line? Are you creating a movie? So many options are available, dear ones. What are you wanting? "Elohim of Third Ray," Krista wanting to know. We are Elohim of the Third Ray, yes.

Katherine: Orion is?

Elohim: Some of us are Orion.

Katherine: So are we speaking with the Elohim now?

Elohim: Yes. Elohim of the Third Ray.

Katherine: What is your function?

Elohim: Orion energy, same energy, yes. More clear. Ah! Such a clear talk, now. Very easy to talk with you, now. Yes. How are you?

Katherine: How are you?

Elohim: Yes, we are enjoying this process immensely. We are wanting to help you ascend as a human being: Spirit into the human-angel template. Beautiful angels you are, in this physical reality.

Katherine: So we are human-angels?

Elohim: You are all human-angels, yes.

Katherine: Well, what do you think of this book idea?

Elohim: It will help many people remember who they are. Those who resonate with this book will say, "This is truth. I can feel into the truth of this book. I'm so happy I bought this book. It reminds me of who I am." This is the energy of the book.

Katherine: Will you help us with the book, please?

Elohim: Yes, of course.

Katherine: Thank you. We were discussing, of course, the different elements of the book, and how it will benefit people in their human lives.

Elohim: You must remember that a book is a wonderful block of energy. It contains so many ideas. Do not worry about all the topics being correct, you see. Not everyone is interested in every single chapter. Perhaps one year, they will read one chapter, and the next, they will read another one. It will help them. Certain aspects of the book will resonate. When you purchase a book it is not because the entire book is making sense or is in alignment with your beliefs however there are sections in the book that will create amazing responses within certain individuals. Yes, when they are reading a certain page, "Oh, it is a coincidence! I read this chapter, oh my goodness, I have always wondered about this topic. This is explaining what is going on within me. I love this book. I buy it for all of my family members, now. I love this book. Thank you so much." You do not understand, you do not see the opportunities available to you but with a book it is information shared with many, many people — a wonderful way to create on this planet. Wonderful because many are wanting books. Yes, many are also wanting lectures, but many do not have access to your information. Many are not online, you see. Many are not on the telephone. A book is a physical thing. A book can travel places, as information does.

Katherine: What do you think of having a recorded book?

Elohim: What a wonderful idea. This is new and Krista is quite excited about this book. Yes, you understand that the energy of the word is something that people will resonate with.

Katherine: An audio book.

Elohim: That is a wonderful, interesting option Katherine, good idea. Yes, we believe that it is an additional challenge, however, something quite do-able. Yes.

Session 14

Katherine: Are there spaceships around Sedona?

Orion Council: Yes, many, yes.

Katherine: I had a question about star tetrahedrons, the Merkaba, and axiatonal lines. Do you care to comment on those?

Orion Council: Yes. Star tetrahedrons are a way to engage with the other realms. It is tapping into the wisdom of the other realms. Yes, it is conducting the awakening process. It is amplifying your light sent from itself and it is receiving as well. Yes. It is a form of energy that allows reception and sending of energy.

Katherine: The difference between that and the Merkaba?

Orion Council: The Merkaba is a system of light. It is how life creates unto itself. It is how life creates unto itself.

Katherine: Is it something that is in need of being activated?

Orion Council: Not necessarily. You will simply remember it. A system of knowledge and wisdom, interplaying with the realities available to all. It is a system, very fine system. Different paths for energy to flow. Have different meanings for different energies. The way energy is flowed and directed is key. When you flow it in a certain way, you have a result. A cause and effect. It is an energy exchange.

Katherine: Can you perhaps give an example, for purposes of illustration?

Orion Council: Yes. There are many beings in your galaxy that are fascinated with your life energy. They are wanting to know the dynamics of it all and they are wanting to acclimate [to] the energies of your planet. So they access the grid for information. They are allowed this because they have a benevolent intention, so they are able to read the Earth history and they will understand why humans have come up to this certain point and when they are accessing this history of the world they access the Merkaba.

Katherine: Of the Earth?

Orion Council: Yes.

Katherine: As there is a macrocosm as well as microcosm, so there is a planetary Merkaba, Galactic, or Cosmic Merkaba, like that?

Orion Council: You can separate this way if you'd like. Yes.

Katherine: Just for purposes of understanding.

Orion Council: Yes.

Katherine: Thank you. Axiatonal lines?

Orion Council: They are lines for communication between different levels of intelligence. For intelligence to be understood by those who do not speak the language, you use axes. And so, the other one simply needs to access this axis, and they will also understand and interpret the lesson, the message. They can communicate like telephone, or something like this. They will be able to understand what the other has explained, but in their own language. It is like a transmitter of the energies. It is a transmitter of energies.

Katherine: When you say languages, for example, do you mean languages of light?

Orion Council: Exactly.

Katherine: Oh, I see, thank you. Those were all the question we had for you this evening. Would you like to continue now on the process of Ascension?

Orion Council: Many beings this time on Earth are still not aware of who they are. Many beings on this Earth are wanting to access their Divine potential, wanting to know that they are truly Spirit beings in human form. They simply cannot remember at this moment. The energies now are forcing them to remember, awaken. That is the promise of Ascension. Everyone will know who they are. By the time the Ascension is complete, if they do not recall they will have to continue their Ascension elsewhere. Many are not aware, but they are knowing without words that they are something so much more than their physical bodies. Unexplainable events happening: more miracle stories, more books, more articles, more angel stories, etc., will happen, UFO sightings and so on. The mass media is slowly catching on to this. Slowly, angel stories will become real, and so, one fine day, when science proves that angels exist, it will open up a whole new level of study and your schools will change and the people on your planet will have a completely different perception of one another. It is a wide-scale change: politics running with integrity and no insurance company, only mutual benefits and sharing.

Katherine: Heaven on Earth.

Orion Council: No lending and borrowing, only giving to those who need the most, trading, and so on. That is a potential. After twenty years, Ascension should be complete.

Katherine: Twenty years!

Orion Council: Should be complete in twenty years. That is a prediction, now.

Katherine: Yes, but that means that this period of transition is a lengthy one for humans, in a sense.

Orion Council: Yes, it is, but you do not know how rapidly you are changing the "now."

Katherine: Oh, that's a good thing. I was reading a particular article this morning, about Ascension and it discussed the different levels of the light body and some of them involved extreme headaches as the pituitary opens, the third eye opens, physical changes, like that. And I was wondering if what I read is accurate.

Orion Council: There are a few going through tremendous change. Some will still continue their lessons elsewhere. Some will vibrate at a completely different level. They are wanting things they have not wanted before. Many are accessing the light quotient within. They use it in the waking state to create that which they want for themselves. Just as others use images to play into, others use images to [create] in the new energy. When you facilitate Heaven-On-Earth you have many different tasks to perform. We say not to worry, dear ones, all will be ready in due time. It is Law.

Katherine: So, I take it that means it varies with the individuals.

Orion Council: Yes.

Katherine: So, the raising of the light quotient —

Orion Council: It must be done through intention. Intending for it to happen, makes it happen.

Katherine: How can the angels and archangels help us with that?

Orion Council: You must ask them for their help, first. You will have the intention and they will help. They will pour the light into your energy field. They will integrate their energies within your field if you are wanting this to happen.

Krista: I saw your ram again, Mom, your animal. It had really long horns, curling back. It looked like a ram with really long horns. Right around your feet. It was light brown with short hair and white underneath.

Katherine: Maybe the Council can tell us who that was.

Orion Council: Yes, you have help. You have infused this energy within yourself, because it was mentioned that you can incorporate these attributes. And you can help facilitate the movement of this kind of creature within yourself. You have had experience with these creatures before. You have lived with such creatures before. Lived with such creatures, before, yes?

Katherine: All right.

Orion Council: All right. You enjoyed these creatures and so, you carry their energy because you love them so much. You love them so much.

Katherine: What is their energy?

Orion Council: What is it like? What is the quality of it?

Katherine: Yes, I'd like to know.

Orion Council: It is a soothing energy. It is a knowing of awareness. Aware of your surroundings and aware of who you are interacting with, trying different things. Also, not staying in one place, constantly on the move. Wanting to charge ahead and be brave. Enjoying the moment but continually moving, expanding.

Katherine: Sounds like a ram, a mountain goat. Is this the creature that you spoke of before?

Orion Council: Yes.

Session 15

Katherine: Here we are in the afternoon, in our backyard.

Krista: Well, it's easy for them to pop in.

Orion Council: You are quite ready to discuss Ascension, yes?

Katherine: But of course!

Orion Council: How is it that the human being does not know who he or she is? At times, you are all questioning who you are. This is a part of the Ascension program. The first stage is recalling your past memories. Yes, recalling your past memories.

Katherine: Of this and other lifetimes?

Orion Council: Well, yes.

Katherine: So there is value in knowing that?

Orion Council: Yes, there is much value in that, yes.

Katherine: What's the second stage?

Orion Council: There are many stages. Like the process of evolution. First you must learn to stand up, then you can walk, then you can run. First, you are aware of who you are. Perhaps this is in the form of recalling past life memories or hypnotizing yourself to remember, or requesting Akashic Readings, or perhaps you will discuss these potential pasts with another one. It is all happening now. You are all feeling drawn to this, because it is a part of the Ascension Program. You will remember in your dream state. You will recall through books. You will watch programs. You will discuss it with other like-minded individuals. And you will do many things. You have your own ways but you will create it for yourselves because it is something you are wanting to do. You are feeling quite attracted to these past lives.

Katherine: Do we ultimately have to discard that or move on, or release the so-called past?

Orion Council: No, it is a tool. You will use what you have learned in the past. You will use those strengths you have developed in the past and use them in this lifetime. You will see what you have yet to develop and if there is anything to develop [that] you chose this lifetime because there were opportunities to be seized. You wanted to seize certain opportunities and they are all available to you at this time. It is a question of seeing, are these the opportunities or illusion? That is the task: illusion or opportunity. Illusion or opportunity.

Katherine: That is the question — which do we seize. Can you help us with the Akashic Reading?

Orion Council: Well, quite difficult without the knowledge. Well, you would have to recall many lifetimes. It is a task, quite a task. You would have to recall many of these past events. Do not worry because it is something innate, but it requires practice to fine-tune the information coming through.

Katherine: So, is Krista capable of channeling that information at this point?

Orion Council: Partial, only partial information. You would want the entire scope. You would want a reading, yes. You would want to know from at least two sources. You would want to know, compare with two sources.

Katherine: Can you guide us how to meet those?

Orion Council: Yes, of course.

Katherine: That would be wonderful. Authentic.

Orion Council: It would help you quite a lot with your progress. It would speed up things for you. It would be a satisfying experience, worthwhile, and worth your investment, yes.

Katherine: While we're on that subject of investment, is it worth our time and money to have these psychic readings here and there, the way we have in the past or is it time now to really focus in very specific ways?

Orion Council: Good question, good question. Well, as you know, all is done in service and the question is "Am I in balance or not in balance?" So, when you are feeling depleted or you are wanting confirmation of the support you have around you, you will most likely get a psychic reading done, to know you have a support system and who is your support system. Also, you would want to do bodywork because perhaps you have [an] ailment in other parts, but we do not advise that you receive much bodywork at this time. More of a fine-tuning of the mind. The mind needs work, now. The energy work is not quite necessary. Not at this moment. Releasing the old habits and so a new paradigm, will set off these events. When you release, a chain of events will be set off — once you

167

release a creative belief. You will attract new experiences due to the released belief. You will attract new experiences to create a new belief about something. Indeed, you previously did not have similar perception.

Katherine: What are some techniques to release old beliefs that no longer serve us?

Orion Council: Well, when you recall the painful events, you can ask them or Self, "Was it correct of me to perceive it in this fashion?" You can say, "Was my perception of it correct or incorrect? What is the truth?" Well, indeed you are asking the right questions because you are intuitively wanting confirmation. You are sensing that it is possible to change your mind to an awakened mind.

Katherine: Yes, and I understand very clearly, intellectually, that it is a question of releasing old, worn-out beliefs. For me the question is always how to release them, especially when much of the material is held in the unconscious.

Orion Council: Do not worry about clearing the right "junk out of the trunk." Do not worry about clearing the correct pieces to be a perfect one. It is not necessary. You must relax into this new energy.

Katherine: But didn't you just say a moment ago that it is important to release old habits?

Orion Council: Yes it is, but you must relax into the new energy.

Katherine: Can you elaborate on what that actually means?

Orion Council: Sometimes the human being is not aware of the opportunities they have. They simply sit and feel stuck. They feel as if they cannot move left or right. In this new energy you have so many opportunities, you must feel as if you are in a playground — an infinite playground. There are many different kinds of games to play and to choose from. When you are observing, you are not choosing, you are not participating. You are simply observing. Accept this fact that you are observing the playground. Feel content within yourself that you are observing. That is all.

Katherine: But if we simply observe "what is" then do we not create more of what already is?

Orion Council: When you are observing, you are researching your possibilities as well. It is like a detailed study of the opportunities you could take. You could take it forward, you could go into depth about these opportunities available to you. You could study them for ten years. Where do you want to be, dear one? Do you want to observe for the next ten years? We do not think so. We think that you actively want to participate in creating. This is why many of you are not feeling quite right because you are not creating. Katherine, this is for you, dear one. You must remember your ability to create. You must also appreciate that which you have created before and you will see you are creating right now. Yes, you are correct: that which you observe now you will create more of. This is why it is important to avoid distractions as you notice yourself in your own life what is a distraction to you and what is not. You have the choice in every moment, Katherine, dear one. It is your choice, if it is a distraction, it is, if it is not, it is helpful. It is up for you to decide for yourself.

Katherine: In the present moment?

Orion Council: Yes. Do not worry about the other ones. You have choices to make for yourself. What are you wanting for yourself? You must ask this question or you will simply observe. Are you wanting to participate in events? Are you wanting to communicate with another one? Are you wanting to create more artwork or something of a light nature? Are you wanting to focus on health and being an energized being? We are saying that when you focus on what brings you joy, you become more energized. You will feel more vitality and the health that is innate within you. You have optimum health already when you participate in the things that bring you joy. You are accessing this health that you already have. It is not outside of you, dear one. You see, when you find those things that bring you joy, you will feel actively engaged in your present moment and you will see the path clearly because you have allowed the channels to be open within yourself from your waking mind to your subconscious mind, to your Higher Self. That is the path of joy. When they say it is actually a path, it is from the Higher Self to the subconscious, to the waking self. That is a path of joy.

Katherine: Is that the path that it always follows?

Orion Council: Well, as you observe, so does the Higher Self. Are you receiving information from your Higher Self or are you receiving information from your environment? It is an interesting age-old question. Who directs whom? Where do these ideas come from?

Katherine: Is it not both?

Orion Council: Many human beings are not aware of the opportunities available to them. They think that what they need is outside of themselves, but when they are truly creating themselves, that is what they are actively doing.

Katherine: Drawing from the Higher Self?

Orion Council: It is not a one-way avenue. It is a combination of the perceived and the received information — received from the Higher Self, perceived within the environment and it is understood in the brain.

Katherine: So it is both?

Orion Council: Yes. We call it "observing." Yes it is constant work, yes, it is lightwork. Yes, you are doing good unto yourself and others but you have to remember that you are observing or participating in the game.

Katherine: Are we not doing both, observing and participating; sometimes one and sometimes the other?

Orion Council: What we mean is, when you are participating, you are involved in that which brings you joy.

Katherine: Yes, and when observing, one is standing on the sidelines? Is that it?

Orion Council: Do not worry, dear one. The time will come when you say, "Ah, this is what I enjoy most." You will feel the sensation within your entire being. You will know what to do next.

Katherine: That is what I pray for.

Orion Council: Yes. You are creating this kind of event for yourself. You are in the lull and you are wanting a surge of clarity.

Katherine: Yes, that's right.

Orion Council: Yes, that is what you are creating. Congratulations, it is going to happen to *you*.

Katherine: Thank you. And I will thank you again when I am in the midst of it. Why do we have these lulls? Is it a chance to turn things over — clear out junk in the trunk, as you said? Are these valuable moments?

Orion Council: You are either in the flow of things or not. Sometimes the current is quite fast, is it not? Sometimes it is slow and soft. There are different vibrations. But the question is: are you going with the flowing of Your Being?

Katherine: The only indicator of that, are feelings?

Orion Council: You must remember to activate the chakra system. How does it feel in my physical vicinity? How does it feel in my inner organs? How does it feel on my skin? How does it feel? Is it something that is engaging my mind? Is it something that makes me feel connected to All-that-Is? Are my senses being stimulated and am I enjoying the future possibilities of what I am doing in this moment? What is a future potential of this actively engaging in a task? Does it have a future potential? You are enjoying projects, dear one. You enjoy projects very much. We have said this before. You enjoy the entire act of facilitating a project and seeing the different aspects of the projects. You do not simply want to be the writer, you want to be the planner. You want to be the time-keeper and the treasurer. You enjoy all of these tasks.

Katherine (Laughing): And director.

Orion Council: Correct. So, dear one, we leave you with these words: what do you want? Goodbye.

Katherine: Goodbye and thank you. An abrupt departure!

Session 16

Krista: "11-11-11"

Katherine: *Woo hoo!*

Orion Council: Well, hello friend. It has been a while. How are you?

Katherine: Very well, fine to speak with you again.

Orion Council: It is nice to be here. Many are wanting to talk with you.

Katherine: Are all of the Council there?

Orion Council: All.

Katherine: All eight of you?

Orion Council: Yes.

Katherine: Where is the training officer?

Orion Council: They are here. They are training officers. Many of us want to talk with you.

Katherine: Go ahead. Please do — about Ascension. Yes?

Orion Council: Ascension is happening now. You have to remember who you are.

Katherine: Yes. Magnificent Beings of Light.

Orion Council: Yes, you have remembered, Katherine. Why do you think you did not see what you saw today? You saw something today, Katherine.

Katherine: This morning, I did, indeed.

Orion Council: Yes. It was quite a wonderful experience for you.

Katherine: I'm not quite sure I'm correct in what I saw.

Orion Council: Ah. Might we add onto what you saw?

Katherine: Please do.

Orion Council: An opening of the system was apparent to your waking Self.

Katherine: Those energy swirls?

Orion Council: Well, it was an opening of energy system.

Katherine: I saw something that looked like a "star-burst." I also saw energy patterns, swirls it seemed to me.

Orion Council: Oh, they were energy system opening.

Katherine: Can you elaborate?

Orion Council: Yes. You saw what you needed to see. You needed to see that you have this energy system available to you. You can access it at all times.

Katherine: Wonderful gift!

Orion Council: You see the proof of it.

Katherine: Yes.

Orion Council: Might we add that it was a nice experience for you because it did something you have wanted to witness for a long time.

Katherine: Indeed, I have. The energy system, the opening, was that part of my etheric body, in some way or otherwise?

(Recording stopped)

Orion Council: Do not worry, friends, it is all right. "We can repeat lessons," Krista says. When you remember who you are, magic happens.

Katherine: Yes, magic happens. So, you are feeling exuberant as well?

Orion Council (Enthusiastically): Yes!

Katherine: Vortices opening all around the world?

Orion Council: Oh yes, many are open now.

Katherine: Now, what will this mean for human-angels?

Orion Council: Ah, you have begun to use a new term.

Katherine: Yes. You like it?

Orion Council: Yes. Quite correct. No longer humans — *human-angels*.

Katherine: More specific, closer to the truth.

Orion Council: Closer to this new title, yes. My, you are beautiful. So beautiful. So beautiful, you are. So many colors. So many lifetimes. So much wisdom. So much to offer others.

Katherine: Thank you. I feel a step closer to the truth of who I am.

Orion Council: Because you saw some things today, perhaps?

Katherine: I think that added to it, yes.

Orion Council: Well done.

Katherine: If it's possible, I really would like to gain more information or elaboration on what it was. Krista and I were saying "soul star chakra" (these energetic patterns), but I'm not sure if that's accurate. Could you shed any light on that, if you'll pardon the pun?

Orion Council: Orange energy opening within you, now. Orange energy. Orange energy opening within you now.

Katherine: And what does the orange signify?

Orion Council: Yes, Metatronic energy.

Katherine: Oh, Metatron!

Orion Council: Yes. Metatron, yes. Has always been with you, Metatron.

Katherine: Is this The Council speaking, or Metatron?

Orion Council: Orion Council, here.

Katherine: *High* Council of Orion.

Orion Council (Joking): Yes. It is not low council.

(Laughter)

Orion Council: You have a connection with Metatron. Energy connection. What you saw today was an example of what you have in your energy field. You have many layers to your energy field. You saw one part of it. You have beautiful colors, so many colors.

Katherine: Well that sounds like a very good thing.

Orion Council (Speaking rapidly): Of course. You are only good. You are ready for the next step. You are ready for the next change. You are ready for the next thing. You are ready for the next way to life. You are ready for a new beginning. You are ready for new people. You are ready for a change. You are ready to make change in your life. You are ready for all of humanity to awaken. You are ready for the shift to complete!

Katherine: *Bring it on!*

Orion Council: You are ready, yes, you are. Okay, yes. Well done, well done. Well done, dear one, well done.

Katherine: Thank you.

Orion Council: Party here, with us.

Katherine: You know, it was so interesting, that energy field opening. There was no color to it at all, it just seemed like grays or black and white. It was a bit of a welcome surprise. I was looking at the ceiling and didn't discern any colors, it was sort of like shadows. Very interesting.

Orion Council: Many beings are with you. Remember that as well.

Katherine: I am remembering my angels and remembering to ask them for things and to thank them.

Orion Council: Good.

Katherine: And I am seeing evidence of things asked for. I got a perfect parking space today, thank you.

Orion Council: Thank your own Self. Who created that? Michael?

Katherine: Oh, I did ask Michael.

Orion Council (Slyly): Oh? *Was it* Michael?

Katherine: You are tempting me to rethink some things, here.

Orion Council: Oh, yes.

Katherine: You say that we are powerful Beings of Light, powerful Creators, creating our experience in every moment. So, how does asking our angels for assistance, fit in with what we create for ourselves? Should we be looking at ourselves and saying "I create this and that" rather than giving "props" to our angelic helpers? What are you suggesting?

Orion Council: There is a difference between gratitude and respect. There is a difference.

Katherine: Please, define the two for us.

Orion Council: Gratitude is giving thanks to another, saying to them they have done service. Respect is, well, somewhat dis-information. There is dis-information with respect. It is not "Who I appreciate." What is respect? You say to someone, "I respect you, I respect your work." Is it thanks? It is separation. Respect is separation. Many are respecting something greater than who they are.

Katherine: Is that wrong, or not the appropriate —

Orion Council: Well, no one is greater than the other. How can you respect when all are equal?

Katherine: Well, in our human-angel terms, respect can be shown to those whom you consider your equals. "I respect you, even though I disagree with you." "I respect you as a fellow human being "or "I respect you as an intelligent being." I don't think it is automatically propping someone up higher. I think respect can be someone with whom you are on par.

Orion Council: Respect creates a space between two. Respect does not want to touch the other. Respect wants to be separate. "You do your work, I do mine." It is separation energy. "I respect your space." "I respect your property." "I do not come onto your property." "I do not play in your playground, I respect your playground." When the angels help you, do you respect them?

Katherine: I feel gratitude. I do feel respect also. Well, when I speak to you, I feel respectful.

Orion Council: Yes, you create a separation.

Katherine: So what would be the opposite of respect? What word?

Orion Council: Communion.

Katherine: *Oh!* Communion with Source! Yes!

Orion Council: Yes, Katherine. Communion. Oneness.

Katherine: That touches my heart.

Orion Council: Yes. Respect: "I respect God," [or] "I am One with God." "I respect angels" [or] "I am one with angels."

Katherine: I understand now, thank you.

Orion Council: You are the one to create so much. Be at one with yourself. Love yourself. "I love myself. I take care of myself. I am one with myself. I am my best friend. I love myself and I take care of myself. I am a part of the whole. I am important. I nurture my energy field."

Katherine: Now I fully understand the difference. Thank you for clarifying.

Session 17

(Editor's note: Krista feels extremely tired and wants to sleep.)

Katherine: Eleven, eleven, eleven. Come on Krista, it's party time. Tell the "munchkins" to help keep you awake!

Orion Council: Well, hello friends. Yes, it is nice to be here again.

Katherine: Welcome.

Orion Council: Well, thank you. Yes, you have "munchkin" friends everywhere. Cannot see the floor there are so many here.

Katherine: Are they Krista's friends?

Orion Council: Well, yes. Well, we are joking but there are a few of them here.

Katherine: Well, maybe they can help keep her alert.

Orion Council: Alert perhaps. Do not worry.

Katherine: It's all acclimating to the energies?

Orion Council: You must continue to ask us questions.

Katherine: Ah, there's a change of the guard, there. Yes, okay, lots of questions.

Orion Council (Laughing): Funny one, you are.

Katherine: I like to hear you laugh.

Orion Council: Yes, we laugh with you, yes.

Katherine: How can you laugh when you say that you do not have human emotions, like we have human emotions?

Orion Council: It is a way of giving the energy through to you. You can see that it is positive when there is laughter.

Katherine: Oh, I see. I like to make you laugh. Well, please talk more about this magical date, 11-11-11.

Orion Council: Yes, many are training to be lightworkers and many are aware that they are lightworkers. Many more will become aware that they are lightworkers. How lovely.

Katherine: Yes, more light, more light, more light.

Orion Council: Yes, and more will awaken to who-they-truly-are. It is not something that is over and done with. There is still so much more happening. There is so much more to you that you do not know. This is why it is so fun to be alive at this moment: continuing to search your Self, who you are, experience who you are, on this planet, why you have come, your past and the possible future. Well, it is only normal because of the intensity of this energy. It is quite intense for the body to hold. It is obtainable but hard to remain in the body, sometimes.

Katherine: Could you perhaps shed some light or under-standing on what happened in the car, when Krista —

Orion Council: Well, yes, it was awakening, it was awakening. Who-you-are comes through, sometimes. Who-you-are is amazing light.

Katherine: She said she felt that she was in an altered state.

Orion Council: Yes, well, her mind was shut off in a sense. Her mind was inactive. Her mind was not available. You understand. Her mind was "out to lunch."

(Laughter)

Orion Council: Her mind was not here. Her mind was sleeping.

Katherine: Yes, her rational mind.

Orion Council: Yes, that one, yes.

Katherine: Okay, so what came through was soul? It seemed like a lot of emotions?

Orion Council: It was another level of her Being. It was angelic part that is awake and awaiting to be expressed. It wants to be expressed. It wants to be acknowledged. It wants attention.

Katherine: Why was it so unhappy?

Orion Council: It wants attention.

Katherine: So its saying, "I want to go home, I want to go home" was to get attention?

Orion Council: Yes.

Katherine: As simple as that?

Orion Council: Not simple, but, well, simple to a certain extent. The mind is turned off and so the angelic part of who she is was trying to tap in and was available to communicate what it wanted to communicate.

Katherine: Are you aware of what was said?

Orion Council: Yes. You have to understand that you have a different perspective of what happened.

Katherine: Was what I said to her helpful at all?

Orion Council: Tremendously.

Katherine: She said that was the third time that that happened to her.

Orion Council: Yes, she has another part of herself that is awaiting to be expressed.

Katherine: I don't know if that frightened her or unsettled her in any way.

Orion Council: Not at all. It was helpful.

Katherine: Thank you. Could you speak about grace, please?

Orion Council: So many here are wanting to communicate, waiting to come in. It is waiting to come in.

Katherine: Well, I would like to hear about grace.

Orion Council: It wants to come in.

Katherine: What wants to come in?

Orion Council: It's so fast.

Katherine: This angelic part of her?

Orion Council: Fast vibration. It's a fast vibration.

Katherine: The Council of Orion?

Orion Council (Krista breathing heavily): Yes. We are here.

Katherine: What's going on?

Orion Council: Well it's not easy to always talk. It's not always easy to talk when you cannot free the Self. It's not easy when the Self is still contained in the vessel [Krista]. Can try to come in more but it's not easy. We want to come in. She wants us to come in. It's not easy at times. It's possible now to come into the vessel. She wants us to come in. She's fine with it. It's so bright in this room. It's so bright. Yes, it is bright in this room. It's so bright in this room.

Katherine: Why do you think it's bright?

Orion Council: It's so bright. It's too bright.

Katherine: Bright from what?

Orion Council: Light. It's a bright light. It's all right, it's all right. We want to come into the vessel and it's happening more...Well, we are coming in. We are coming in. Yes, we want to come into the vessel.

Katherine: Is she saying "okay?"

Orion Council: Yes. But it is not easy. Not easy. It's not easy. That's why light is so strong. It's so strong — white light — it's so strong. It's okay. It's okay.

Katherine: It's okay now?

Orion Council: You are okay. You are fine. Well, it's a lot of energy for a vessel, now. It's a lot of energy for one vessel to contain.

Katherine: What was the fast vibration?

Orion Council: It was us coming in. It's not easy. It's so light. It is better now. It is clear now. Energies are very slow now, in the body, yes.

Katherine: How does it feel in the body?

Orion Council (Laughing): It is amazing. It is so wonderful. How beautiful; a body. It's like a capsule. It is like a capsule. What a beautiful body.

Katherine: Feel your hair.

Orion Council (Laughing, touching Krista's hair): Ha!

Katherine: Feel your face.

Orion Council (Laughing, touching Krista's face): It is so exciting. We have to tell you a few things, but we are so excited to be in the body.

Katherine: Good for you!

Orion Council: Yes. Well, not completely, but much of us here. It is not easy. Well done. Well done.

(Editor's note: Katherine holds Krista's hands)

Orion Council: It is so amazing. Yes. We are flying in a body.

Katherine: Do you feel heavy at all?

Orion Council: Well, not quite. It is unusual.

Katherine: Do you want to sit up?

Orion Council: Not yet, please. Not fully inside. We must focus, first. We must focus before your questions. Yes, well. Grace is a kindness. Grace is a way of behaving towards others who are not awake. It is a state of complete acceptance of one another. Acceptance, yes, acceptance of who they are as well as who you are.

Katherine: What is meant by: "We live by grace, God's grace?"

Orion Council: It is when you ask for God to be present, you activate a potential for the whole of Earth to be surrounded by intervening of grace.

Katherine: I'm sorry, could you repeat that?

Orion Council: When you ask God for help, you ask grace energy to intervene with a probable planet. Grace is like a tool of God; a tool to dismantle that which does not work any longer. It melts hearts.

Katherine: Are angels present, today? Oh, they are always present. Are there angels in the room who want to come forward?

Krista: Mom, I'm trying, it just feels like my heart's beating a lot.

Katherine: Do you know what happened? Did you feel them come in? How did that feel to you?

Krista: It was nice, I could feel sensations all over. I could feel many parts of my body at one time and I had to stay really still.

Katherine: That's a lot of energy coming into your body.

Krista: It's like at the dentist, one of those lights over your head.

Katherine: That bright light?

Krista (Suddenly shouting): Oh!! I got a jolt of energy. That's what I got once when I had healing work done.

Katherine: You had healing done?

Krista: Yes. I asked Michael to. I wanted it to be removed from the top.

Katherine: There you go, you got your answer.

Krista: It's still there. I can ask it. Yes, it's there.

Katherine: Do you want it gone?

Krista: Yes, I want the block gone. Oh, ho, ho. It feels like a huge vacuum or something.

Katherine: Let it go.

Krista: It's kind of shocking when it happens, though.

(Krista gets another jolt, shouts and begins to laugh.)

Katherine: Is that Michael?

Krista (Laughing): Yes, it's like a huge suction cup. I feel it.

Katherine: Do you remember to say thank you? I guess that answers our question if the angels are with us, today.

Krista: Thank you. Oh my gosh, it's really strong, and this light goes on. It's really different now, it goes over my eyes.

Katherine: Is that blockage gone?

Krista: Something's happening, I don't know. It's all over from my heart to my solar plexus, going up. I feel it's really active. There it is again. It's all over. Oh, it's so big, I don't know what it is. It's a huge energy.

Katherine: Positive energy, good feeling?

Krista: Yes.

Katherine: You realize about energy coming into your body; you're getting a lot and it's tiring.

Krista: Yes, that's what it was.

Katherine: It's this energy infusion when channeling.

Krista: Yes. Oh! Surge again.

(Laughter)

Katherine: You just felt that? You look alert now.

Krista: I guess that was an immediate answer.

Katherine: Kodoish, Kodoish, Kodoish, Adonai Tsebayoth. Eyeh Asher Eyeh. I Am that I Am. Nuk pu Nuk. I am the Presence of God. I am a Magnificent Being of Light. I am a Sovereign Being of Light. I Am that I Am. Thank you, Source. One with God is a majority. The place upon where I stand is Holy Ground.

Krista (Seeing a vision): It was so beautiful when you were saying that. I saw a beautiful mountain. Like, if you think of Mount Olympus, marble and light halls. Oh, it's so beautiful, like the sky is just pink and white. These holy, holy beings just all over. They're sort of, just there, floating on different parts of the mountain. They're experiencing, they're just there, this holy, pure, pure place. It's better than any fantasy story or mythical, utopian painting.

Katherine: Because you can feel it.

Krista: If you go there, you don't say anything. It's a beautiful silence that's there. I feel like I saw these gates of heaven.

Katherine: How wonderful; we are definitely celebrating 11-11-11 today!

Krista (Laughing): We are!

Orion Council: Hello, friends.

Katherine: Hello. Welcome. What is happening now?

Orion Council: Energies are intense, today.

Katherine: That's a good thing?

Orion Council: Indeed, it is.

Katherine: All around the Earth, I assume, and beyond — is that correct?

Orion Council: Yes.

Katherine: What Krista experienced, before, she said it was Michael's energy, helping to remove some sort of blockage in her torso area. She said she felt it being pulled or sucked out of her crown. Can you add anything to that and give us some clarity?

Krista: There's much to say Mom, I can't say it.

Katherine: Just relax, just relax.

Krista: Hmm, that helps, it does.

Katherine: That's good. Remember you are safe. You are safe and surrounded by love.

Krista: I'm just seeing so many pictures and it's distracting. The energy seems to just —

Katherine: You have lots of spiritual help, so you can call on your spiritual team if you want some assistance in managing the images, right?

Krista: Yes, why not? Yes. Please God, allow us in the highest good and the healing energy, the angels, angelic beings that are purest of the pure and completely benevolent in their intentions, to go to these people who requested to be on the prayer list. May they receive the highest love and light possible be directed to them at this time and everything will be used for the highest good of all. Thank you. May the Archangels assist us in sending healing energies to these people, thank you.

Session 19

Katherine: Should we start with our prayer, since you are more accepting of it now?

Krista: I guess so, I feel so heavy when they are coming in.

Both: Kodoish, Kodoish, Kodoish, Adonai Tsebayoth.

Orion Council: Well you are already feeling the high vibrations today. Yes. Do not worry, friends. Quiet is needed at this time. Intuition is important to remember. Many have told Krista to be quiet. She knows. Time to be quiet. Go within today. Go within today, please. No time for discussion, today. Too much discussion has happened. Need to look within, today. You must remember what is happening — happening inside of yourselves, not on the outside. Changes are occurring, now.

Katherine: It's a beautiful time. When you say "discussion" do mean channeling, or —

Orion Council: Intuition is needed to focus the light within and to gain answers, for everyday living. Must look within.

Katherine: That sounds like good advice at all times. You've always encouraged and admonished us to focus the light within.

Orion Council: Well, yes, you must do it. You have done it, but not enough.

Katherine: Pray without ceasing, as the Good Book says.

Orion Council: Yes, it's a good book, yes. How can you remember who you are if you are not quiet? Remembering who you are is happening, now. Yes?

Katherine: Yes. It's still wonderful to walk the Earth. It's still wonderful to appreciate being a human-angel.

Orion Council: May we suggest laying down and lighting a candle for humanity?

Katherine: We can do that right now.

Orion Council: With the intention of awakening the masses, ask for all to become awake and it shall happen! All you have to do is ask. All you have to do is ask!

Katherine: Ask who, what?

Orion Council: Ask the Council of Orion.

Katherine: To do what?

Orion Council: To awaken humanity!

(Laughter)

Katherine: Council of Orion, please help awaken all of humanity! It's a tall request.

Orion Council: Well, we want to help. Yes, we want to help all.

Katherine: Well, you are helping.

Orion Council: We want to help.

(Krista continues to laugh)

Katherine: Well, Krista, you may lay down. I have a candle lit here, as per their instructions. Council, would that it were so easy just to wave your wand and have humanity awaken —

Orion Council: Yes. We can do this. Yes. We can do this. We can awaken humanity, together, we can.

Katherine: Well, let us get to it.

Orion Council: Oh it is so wonderful to be in a body. Aha! What joy. What a joyful feeling to be in a body.

Katherine: Do you still feel as if you are the capsule?

Orion Council: Yes. We are here. Ah, ha, ha, ha! Nice to be in a body with you.

Katherine: Nice to have you here.

Orion Council: Hello.

Katherine: Hello.

Orion Council: It is a nice day. Yes. Ha, ha ,ha, ha. Want some cake?

Katherine: Well, that will be later. *(Ed. note: referring to our birthday cake.)*

Orion Council: We would like to try some cake.

Katherine: Well, definitely, you may.

Orion Council: We are joking. It is not of importance.

Katherine: Actually, since you are in the body, can you taste?

Orion Council: Well, of course we are sharing an experience, now.

Katherine: Would you like to taste a bit of tea?

Orion Council: No. Thank you.

(Laughter)

Katherine: Impeccably polite.

Orion Council: Yes. Yes. Hello.

Katherine: Hello. What do you see?

Orion Council: We do not "see."

Katherine: Well, you're in the body?

Orion Council: Ah. Ah.

Katherine: Can you open Krista's eyes?

Orion Council: No. It is not comfortable. She has too many distractions.

Katherine: Well, when the time comes for you to open your eyes you might be so shocked you charge out of it.

(Laughter from both)

Katherine: Well, we have the candle lit, here. Now, what was the next part of what you —

Orion Council: Well, now we must ask for all of humanity to awaken. "Please God," say, "Please help."

Katherine: "Please, God, please help —"

Orion Council: "We want to awaken humanity to who they are."

Katherine: "We want to awaken humanity to who they are."

Orion Council: "Thank you."

Katherine: "Thank you, Source."

Orion Council: Yes. We are glad to have this experience with you because it would be meaningless if we only freed the mind and not the whole soul. We want to free the soul as well. We want to help you free your souls from the limitations of the Earth. You live with the belief system that tells you that you cannot do certain things without money or cars or other such things, but you, of course understand, you create everything yourself. For you yourself attract the vibrational essence of what you want and you have an idea of what kind of experience you are wanting. Cars are details. It is not so much the car as it is the experience of driving on the highway that one is wanting. That is how you attract a car. You imagine yourself driving it. How does it feel? "Such a cliché now," Krista says.

Katherine: True, nonetheless, accurate, nonetheless. How does it smell? How does it sound? And all of the toys inside the car — the CD players —

Orion Council: Yes.

Katherine: — and the comfortable seats and —

Orion Council: Exactly.

Katherine: — the sun roof and the light coming in through the top.

Orion Council: Yes.

Katherine: Is it accurate to say that once we've followed through on that process of feeling, we need to not contradict ourselves half an hour later by saying, "Oh, that's not possible, I can't," isn't that so?

Orion Council: We understand it takes time and practice for you humans because you have so many distractions. We can only give the lesson to you. You must implement it into your own lives. That is the work to be done; learning to work with these teachings. If someone told you that the sky was green, you would have to unlearn many things. You would have to unlearn what you believe about vision and colors and the science of the waves and so on. Unlearning as well as learning, in a sense.

Katherine: I think that's why it's a bit challenging because we're unlearning outmoded beliefs. We've talked about core beliefs before. It is always a question of belief.

Orion Council: Yes. It is always a question of what you are wanting and what you think you can have.

Katherine: I want to believe that I can be, have, and do everything. I think you defined that as one part of Ascension: a knowingness; knowing the truth of our Being. That is the truth, isn't it?

Orion Council: Yes, dear one. You have the power to create an entire universe but you do not believe that you can. You do not simply believe that you can do this. That is the question. *We* can tell you this, but you would not believe it because you have to unlearn many things. You are your own limitation. That is why we ask to free the soul. We speak of truth and the humans recognize this truth intuitively, then they begin the process of concentrating on these truths, in their waking state, and as they find evidence supporting these truths, they begin to unlearn. That has been the pattern. A new truth, then see evidence of it, and then implementing that truth in one's life.

Katherine: Are you suggesting there is an alternative way?

Orion Council: Of course there is magic and of course there is miracle and prayers and manifesting with intention of many at the same time and so on. When you are in numbers, of course the intention is there and so powerful changes may happen when you complete such transmissions in groups.

Katherine: Therein lies their value?

Orion Council: Yes, one hundred lightworkers can overcome millions of, millions, who are destructive upon the planet. One hundred lightworkers could shift the energy for one million people with the intention held, to heal or something like this.

Katherine: Yes. Critical mass. How do we attract to ourselves, like-minded lightworkers to our experience?

Orion Council: You simply ask and you follow intuition. Do those things you are wanting to do. Within your society, you know best.

Katherine: Ask of whom, Higher Self?

Orion Council: You know best.

Both Krista and Katherine light a candle for the waking of humanity.

Session 20

Orion Council (Joking): You missed the introduction to us.

Katherine (Joking): How about an instant replay?

Orion Council: Do not worry, friends. It is time to discuss Ascension. Yes, are you ready to discuss Ascension?

Katherine: Yes, always.

Orion Council: Well! Hello.

Katherine: Hello, I just need to say the date.

Orion Council: Yes, you need to say the date.

Katherine: Do you know what it is?

Orion Council: It's the sixteenth of November.

Katherine (Checking the calendar): The sixteenth?

Orion Council: Yes. Do not worry, friends, it is the sixteenth of November, *1985!*

(Laughter)

Orion Council: Do not worry friend, time does not exist.

Katherine: That's right, time does not exist.

Orion Council: No. How are you? We love you. How are you?

Katherine: Loving you, too!

Orion Council: Yes, it is good to be here. It is wonderful to speak with you. We want to discuss Ascension.

Katherine: Please do.

Orion Council: How are you today?

Katherine: Happy.

Orion Council: All right. It is nice to speak with you again. Hello. You are beautiful! How are you?

Katherine: Wanting to hear about Ascension.

Orion Council: Okay. Today is a beautiful day. Many lightworkers are wanting to raise consciousness. You see, this example with the books here at the table *(Ed. note: a collection of "New Age" books.)* Many are wanting to raise their energies. They are wanting to know about the possibility for the soul's evolution. They want to become some sort of Enlightened Beings of the Light. Oh dear. Now is not the time to become Ascended Masters. So what!

(Laughter)

Orion Council: What is an Ascended Master? Someone in a white cloak? Oh, come on!

(More laughter)

Orion Council: Do you want to be an Ascended Master? What do you want to be? Come on?

Katherine: Is that a direct question?

Orion Council: Yes.

Katherine: Well, no, I do not want to be an Ascended Master.

Orion Council: What do you want to be, then?

Katherine: I want to be one who communes with Source.

Orion Council: Well, you are. What else do you want?

Katherine: <u>Consciously</u> to commune with Source.

Orion Council: Aha! A Conscious Creator.

Katherine: That's it. Every minute, aware.

Orion Council: It is very possible. You are a Conscious Creator in every moment. Of course, the goal of the game is to remember who you are. The goal of the game is to focus on the light within. That is the goal: to bring the Heaven onto the Earth. You are working on this, friend. You are an example to all. You do this naturally. It is your state of being. You do this naturally. "Your natural state of being, to use your own words," Krista says. She is using your own words. Stolen words –

(Laughter)

Orion Council: However, you are a Conscious Creator. You come from the Light. You carry the Light. It is within your Self and you give it to all around you and so on and so on. The Light continues to flow through you. You are doing a service onto God by focusing the light upon others as well as your Self. Ascension is remembering this process. Ascension is walking around the bagel store, remembering you are a lightworker. Ascension is about remembering you are from home and discussing that with other people, not necessarily awake but, bit by bit, they become awake as well. They are wanting to become awake. They are wanting to see proof. So many say, "If only there were proof I would believe in heaven, I would not believe in hell anymore. I live in hell," they say. "This is hell, oh dear!" And they have no idea how badly they wanted to come to this Earth. Why would you want to come here, if it were hell? Dear one, you see what we mean by this?

Katherine: Of course, of course.

Orion Council: How can they say, "It is hell" when they were *fighting* to come here, almost.

(Laughter)

Orion Council: Not in that sense, but "Whoa, let me go to the plane of the physicality, please! God, please!"

(More laughter)

Orion Council: They prayed and the soul...okay. Now they complain about the hell on Earth. It is not quite understandable from our perspective, however you are the ones experiencing. You tell us. How is it here? We do not want you to answer that question but it is all right because we know what you really think, ha, ha, ha! Do you understand our joke?

Katherine: No.

Orion Council: We commune with your Highest Self.

Katherine: Oh, okay, so you already know.

Orion Council: Yes. Your Highest Self loves it here. Your Higher Self knows everything. Oh, the beauty of it all; if only you could see from our perspective how beautiful you are. Dear one, you think beauty is one flower, one rose. How about a multidimensional rose that extends to All-that-Is, touched by the Light of God, experiencing the many lifetimes? Oh, more colors than the ones you see now, more songs, the most beautiful music, angel voices — that is all you. You do not understand; we can only give you hints. Language is so limited; it cannot describe how beautiful you are. Oh, it is so beautiful. Oh, the light, oh the light you are shining now, if you could only see it. You could tap into this, if you were to meditate, you could get a hint of this beauty that you are.

Katherine: You summed it up perfectly.

Orion Council: We love talking with you. You are a beautiful Creator.

Katherine: Thank you.

Orion Council: We want you so desperately to remember this.

Katherine: And I want to remember.

Orion Council: You will. You are. When you focus the light within, God is saying how much God loves you. You are God. You are All-That-Is. You are the wind. You are the fire, the Earth and the water. You are all of that, *That Is*. You are so beautiful. Can you see it, dear one?

Katherine: I can feel it a little bit.

Orion Council: Yes, you are remembering. It will happen more and more so. If you think a rose is beautiful, and we tell you, it is even more beautiful than what you are experiencing it as now. You would be amazed at what you would see.

Katherine: Didn't we agree to the game, the forgetting game?

Orion Council: You did, but you are now beginning to remember home, while in physicality. The whole universe is overwhelmed. The angels are crowding in. The angels are everywhere. Angels all over the place.

(Laughter)

Orion Council: Too many angels, now.

Krista: Mom, I feel like I was going to have a heart attack, almost.

Katherine: Why? Is your heart beating rapidly? Take a deep breath. Tell me what you're feeling.

Krista: I felt like in my heart was taking over — like a fire, like it was going to explode and burst.

Krista (Speaking to Council): Tone it down, guys!

Katherine: Good, Krista, good. You're in control. It's your body. And you're getting all this energy, streaming in.

Krista: Yes, they said in this Pleiadian thing — they said imagine a lotus flower, closing here, on your chakras — if you're going out in a public space. Yeah, that helps, good.

Katherine: That image of the lotus flower helps?

Krista: Yes, closing the chakras down.

Katherine: Oh, okay,

Krista: Oh, it got too intense. I got like a shock. All these books here [in front of us], are high energy books, really high energy books on the table.

Orion Council: We are here. Channel is not quite satisfied with us when we do this, but it is okay. We have an agreement. We have an agreement, you see. We have an agreement, you see, you see?

Katherine: With Krista?

Orion Council: Yes, with Krista. We have an agreement. Okay? You understand?

Katherine: Okay.

Orion Council: Okay? Okay?

Katherine: Yes, yes.

Orion Council: Okay. You understand. We want to make this very clear to you, this is why we keep reiterating. We have an agreement with Krista.

Katherine: So what was that opening?

Orion Council: It was heart. Of course you knew that. It was heart opening. Yes, it is ever more powerful for us to speak with you. I can feel your energy. I can feel your energy. I can. I am Council of Orion Leader.

Katherine: Leader?!

Orion Council: I am a leader, yes. Can you feel it?

Katherine: It feels very, powerful.

Orion Council: Yes. You are connecting with us now, as we speak. We are connecting with your energy field now and we are activating many of your chakras at the moment. You do not know this; your waking Self does not know this. Your unconscious Self is quite aware of what is happening. We are activating many of these. Solar Plexus is active, now. Your solar plexus is becoming more active, now, as we speak.

Katherine: Excellent.

Orion Council: You will recognize a shift in energy as we speak to you, now. You are opening up this vessel that you are, to higher energies now. It is helping you on your path on Ascension — path.

Katherine: Thank you.

Orion Council: You're welcome.

Katherine: I appreciate that, and I feel stronger.

Orion Council: Well, you are strong. That is who you are.

Katherine: I want to remember that.

Orion Council: Yes, do not worry, friend. You will remember. In time you will be fully awake.

Katherine: Very good. Now, what did you mean by you could "read my energy?"

Orion Council: You want to know specific information, yes, Curious One?

Katherine: You know I do!

Orion Council: We are wanting to discuss Ascension.

Katherine: I know; you want to evade the question.

(Laughter from the Council)

Katherine: You know we human-angels, like that.

Orion Council: We are tricky. We are tricky ones.

Katherine: You are very tricky.

Orion Council: Okay, we can discuss anything you would like to discuss with us.

Katherine: How about that last question?

Orion Council: Okay. What is going on in your energy field. You are feeling, sensing the energy of Orion in your field. It is love energy. It's a Christed energy in your field. It is beautiful, a pink, love energy, golden light, white light. Yes. Purple is the color of your angel, now. Your angel, now, is a purple energy.

(Editor's Note: By Christed State or Christ Consciousness, we do not refer to a person or religion. It is a state of spiritualized awareness or illumination and is called by other terms: Heru Consciousness, Cosmic Consciousness, Buddhic Consciousness, etc.)

Katherine: Not a white one, like before?

Orion Council: Not a white one, now. It is purple.

Katherine: Why the change?

Orion Council: It is because active energy has to attune to a different creative force. A different creative force. What you are creating has a different color scheme. Okay?

Katherine: Okay.

Orion Council: It's a color scheme. It is purple now.

Katherine: That's what Krista saw?

Orion Council: Yes. It is purple, in your field. Some of your technology can pick up on colors. Photographs.

Katherine: Yes, Kirlian photography.

Orion Council: Yes. You are aware of it. It's a type of image that is captured in the film. The colors are credited, colors are credited. Colors are credited. Yes?

Katherine: Yes.

Orion Council: It's a good image when you see colors. It tells you what is in your field at the moment.

Katherine: But it changes, doesn't it?

Orion Council: Yes, colors change.

Katherine: That is what people do not understand with the Kirlian photography.

Orion Council: They simply say, "My color is white, all day!"

Katherine: Yes!

Orion Council: Oh no, hello friends. Come on!

Katherine: So, thank you. Now, back to Ascension.

Orion Council: Oh you—tricky! You want to speak what *we* want to speak about. No more questions? Purple energy was kind of angelic, with you. Angelic energy. You had forgotten that you had many angel qualities in your field.

Katherine: What are angelic qualities?

Orion Council: Well, one is you speak like an angel would speak — the sympathy of an angel. Energy of angels in you. Angel of writing. Angel of Orion. Angel of Writing. Angel of Creating. And Angel of Remembering. Yes, many angelic qualities, you have. It is becoming more apparent. It is becoming more apparent. We want to say that at this time many are wanting to experience channeling. Krista is getting an idea. It's to be creating a video, now. What a wonderful thought. We are coming in quite strongly, now. Can we suggest a video?

Katherine: Certainly.

Orion Council: We will come back.

Katherine: Tonight?

Orion Council: In two minutes. Please have a question ready.

Katherine: On channeling or —

Orion Council: Well, a session question. We will record a session. Yes, do not worry, friend. We will work with you. Be careful. Do not ask too important [personal] questions — public eye will see.

Katherine: All right.

Orion Council: We will come back. Don't forget about us. Goodbye.

Katherine: Goodbye.

(Ed. note: The following session was videotaped, as suggested.)

Krista (On camera): I'm laughing because they're here. We didn't prepare this, people! Okay.

Orion Council: Well, hello.

Katherine: Welcome back.

Orion Council: Thank you. We are ready to make a video for all to see us. Hello, friends. We are Orion Council on video.

Katherine: High Council.

Orion Council: High Council, yes, you could say that. How are you today?

Katherine: Just great.

Orion Council: Do not be nervous, friend. You are a professional. Do not worry. We understand that you are a bit nervous because the entire world will see you. But do you know what? An entire other world sees you.

(Laughter)

Orion Council: You understand our humor? Do not worry, friend. Non-physical world sees everything you do. Yes.

Katherine: Well, we do have a question for you.

Orion Council: We are ready for any questions you have for us.

Katherine: How can the channeling that Krista does, benefit lots and lots of people?

Orion Council: That is a wonderful question, a beautiful question from a Creator. Aha! We want to say to ALL, that you are ALL Creators on this planet and it is up to you what you are wanting to create for yourselves. Many at this time are wanting to connect to the Divine Aspect of themselves and we say that you can connect to the Divine Aspect of yourself at any moment, friend.

Katherine: How? We want to know, how?

Orion Council: You will have to ask, simply, and it will happen. It is instantaneous. It is instantaneous. Yes. When you ask to connect, you have the intention first. First you must have desire to connect. You cannot simply say, "I want to do this," and not quite want to do it, friend. You have to want it. You have to want it.

Katherine: Many of the viewers will want to know, "Ask whom?"

Orion Council: Many of you at this time are thinking that the answers lie outside of yourselves. We say, this is not true. The answers lie within your own Self. You own Self has a vast, vast library of information for you to tap into.

215

Many of you have forgotten this fact. We speak to you of the beauty that you are and the love that surrounds you at every moment. We do not talk about the knowledge that surrounds you that you already have contained in your own field. You are also able to connect to the grid, which also holds much information for how the planet is created. We say is created because there is no time, friends — ha, ha — you all know this. We laugh because we enjoy the channel and we enjoy laughing through her. We do not simply laugh, we are all laughter: we are the essence of laughter. We would like to discuss Ascension in the short amount of time that you have. Friends, how can we help?

Katherine: I think it would be useful for the people to know who the High Council of Orion, is?

Orion Council: Orion Council is energy. Orion Council is Divine energy, you could say. We come from Central Sun. We want to discuss Ascension and we come with a Golden Ray. Golden Ray; we come with that. Many angels in the room, as well. Many angels with us. Yes.

Katherine: And can you explain to our viewers, why you say "us?"

Orion Council: We are eight. Eight. Sometimes we are ten, even twelve, but eight most of the time.

Katherine: Well, why did you identify yourselves, just a few moments ago, as "Leader?"

Orion Council: Well, good question, friend. Sometimes we have a different intention, you see. To lead is to introduce a new subject, so we become "Leader." We become one energy but we are eight, because we have focused ourselves in eight different ways.

Katherine: What are the different ways?

Orion Council: Good question, friend. You [have not prepared] for this video however we feel you are quite organized.

Katherine: Thank you.

Orion Council: Well done. Eight different energies with eight different focuses. One main focus is on the love that you are. You are all love energy and we focus on the love that you are. You are beautiful, friend.

Katherine: That's one.

Orion Council: You must see the love energy that you are. Okay, okay. Second one is knowledge energy. You are a knowledge database. You are a database of knowledge — we remind you of that. We give perspectives in the way that we can. We can accumulate knowledge, as well as give knowledge information.

Katherine: That's two.

Orion Council: Yes, what else? We have known you before. It is a remembering — knowledge of remembering who you are. As we have said previously, Angel of Remembering with you at this moment. We do not use names but humans like to use names. Yes, "Bobby" you could say, "Angel Bobby."

(Laughter)

Orion Council: A funny joke. "Angel Bobby of Knowledge" perhaps.

Katherine: So, "remember" is third. What is the fourth?

Orion Council: Communication. We focus on communicating with all that will listen.

Katherine: That's an easier one. And number five?

Orion Council: Well done. Number five is refocusing energy. We want to help you to focus on Ascension.

Katherine: Is that also focusing on the light within?

Orion Council: Yes, correct.

Katherine: So, it's assisting in that?

Orion Council: Yes. We also want to remind you of a sixth: the Energy of Nature. Can you understand? Nature is Energy of the Earth. We have focused on the Earth energy. Six. Energy of Earth. Yes.

Katherine: Okay, and seventh?

Orion Council: It's the energy of the Wisdom of the Ages. Wisdom of the Ages. You could say, "history of the Earth", but we say, "Wisdom of the Ages." Many Ages you have experienced, many ages. Not in one lifetime; many lifetimes, friend. Many lifetimes.

Katherine: On the Earth Plane?

Orion Council: Well, that mostly, for now.

Katherine: What about the other systems in the galaxy?

Orion Council: They will be included. Not important at this moment, for now.

Katherine: And, number eight?

Orion Council: Training you to become more light-focused. We will tell you number nine. Is the Energy of Writing. Writing energy. Creating written memories for the next generation.

Katherine: That's where the book comes in?

Orion Council: Yes.

Session 21

Krista: I feel like they're in my body, right now. I feel very uneasy and uncomfortable and horrible.

Katherine: Well, why don't you ask them for assistance?

Krista: I can hardly concentrate on the happy stories because it's been like this all day.

Katherine: Krista, ask for help. Why don't you ask for help? If you could ask for help, what would you ask for? How would you like to feel?

Krista: I just want to feel happy. I just feel nauseous.

Katherine: Well, ask for help with the nausea.

Krista: Well, is it them? Are they doing that?

Katherine: We could ask, but why aren't you asking for help?

Krista: I don't know! I just want to lay down. That's all I want to do.

Katherine: Lay down, then. Goodness gracious.

Krista: It's being released, or something like that.

Katherine: Okay, there you go.

Krista: What am I supposed to do? I can't talk to anybody about this.

Katherine: Light off, so it's not shining in your eyes. Now, relax. Inhale. Breathe. Yes, that's better.

Krista (Relaxing): I feel like a horrible person.

Katherine: You're not a horrible person, it's just a little discomfort, that's all.

Orion Council: We are here.

Katherine: Welcome.

Orion Council: Hello, friends. It's a nice act of service you are doing. You realize you are doing service work?

Katherine: I'm trying to help her through it.

Orion Council: You are acclimating to the new, well, beginning, yes. New world energies.

Katherine: That's Krista's nausea?

Orion Council: Yes, of course.

Katherine: Can you help to ease it for her?

Orion Council: Yes. We are glad that you are helping and we want to discuss Ascension.

Katherine: Please do.

Orion Council: How can we begin to explain the importance of Ascension? It is a process that is, well, many are undergoing this process. Yes, many at this time are wanting to collaborate and create a mutual understanding in certain spheres. Many are wanting to join together and help shape the planet's energies again, to what it once was before, but a new version.

Katherine: So we are looking forward to a Golden Age — working towards it?

Orion Council: Something like that, yes. It's energy of a new world, new world energy, yes? What are you wanting in the new world? God asks us all. What are you wanting in the new world? That is your role: to determine what you are wanting. Dear ones, you speak of wanting to know what you want for yourself. What a funny question. It is always about what you are wanting to do. You put so much pressure on wanting to know what you want and wanting to know what to do and be and how and when and where. You are not in the moment. You are not simply focusing on what you are wanting to do. You are not allowing yourself to focus in the moment. More and more so we are forced to focus on ourselves in a new way: with a love intention. Any thoughts that are not in accordance with who-you-truly-are will feel quite negative. You will feel the duality of these words when you speak them. You will feel extreme discord when you speak a low vibrational word, because your energies are becoming faster in vibration than they were before. Old habits are not feeling quite so nice. Interesting. What you once thought of as "constructive criticism" is no longer necessary in the new world energy. In the future you will be aiding each other and supporting those positive qualities that you have. You will also have silent time for yourselves — more of this than there was before. Not as much discussion necessary. Much energy work being done. Intuition is increasing on the planet Earth at this time. Many of you are feeling into the new world energies. You are assimilating and becoming new beings, you see. You are no longer the same as before. You are no longer the same as before. You are all becoming Oneness Consciousness and you are also helping each other create their experiences. So, it depends on what you both are wanting: do they match? Do your goals match? That is the new question of relationships at this time. Do our goals match each other's goals?

Katherine: Is it that we can have the same goals and very different ways of approaching them?

Orion Council: That is the game of life. You understand this already. You know, friend, that is the whole game: to lose yourself and relocate yourself.

Katherine: What do you mean by that last comment?

Orion Council: You have lost yourself in duality, now you must find yourself again. Yes, that is the new energy on this planet Earth.

Katherine: Is it accurate to say that when we are talking about new energy, are we talking about the fifth dimension?

Orion Council: Sixth and seventh dimension, even here.

Katherine: Available to us, now?

Orion Council: Yes. Not as many as you would like are in these dimensions, but the larger part of your Self is able to reach a multitude of dimensions.

Katherine: Where are Krista and I, presently?

Orion Council: You are both searching, for answers. You are both searching for validation. You are both searching. You are concerned for the well-being of other people. It is your duty. It is also your vice. You are all constantly focused on others. You seek to help yet it is also your challenge. How does a helper stay balanced when you are programmed to help? Yes, that is not easy for the lightworker. In due time you will see how it all has played out, but at this moment you are wanting validation for all of your beliefs. You want to increasingly have faith in all that you are doing. It is quite normal. You are both wanting respect and appreciation from the fathers but it is also a challenge to make you stronger within your selves. This is why you both chose such people.

Katherine: And not getting it.

Orion Council: Exactly, bingo. Who said it would be an easy game? When will you apply the spiritual truth that all is love? Another challenge: you receive teachings on both levels when you do not see the teacher however, you simply know and you use intuition. Some is trust in intuition. How do those play out in the physical, when you do not see the results of your efforts and how wonderfully you have helped the planet? You would congratulate yourself at every possible moment; you would say, "I have done such a wonderful job."

Katherine: There is a quote from a book, "Love is the answer, now what's the question?"

Orion Council: The question is, "How can I love?" And the answer is, "Love." To simply love is what you do, but the game is "how." The game is "how" love is expressed in this physical world. You can express love in the way that you want. Perhaps your way is to keep things completely organized, looking perfect and shiny. To others, the way of expressing love is to give gifts of items. Some express their love as they listen to other people and spend time with them. Others give love in so many different ways. Others make flower arrangements. This is how they show their love for someone or for a group. There are many different ways. How do you show your love? You know the answer to that one.

Katherine: I'm sure there are as many different ways as there are people and they're all valid.

Orion Council: That is correct. Love is the answer to love. Yes, that is the answer.

Katherine: Can you speak more about "focusing the light within?"

Orion Council: It is like a train running through the tunnel. There is a great accumulation of energy in certain energy centers of the whole body.

Katherine: All assistance is appreciated.

Orion Council: Yes, that is a probability that all will be conducting self-healing in the future.

Katherine: That's wonderful.

Orion Council: When more come together it becomes even more powerful.

Katherine: Yes. Talk about future but we understand that there is no time. Yet, it also seems we are going back to the past, when we were consciously aware of self-healing and assisting others and it's all happening now. Healing temples, right? Healing temples in the past, so-called, past, with crystals, and with light, and with color and sound. Yes?

Orion Council: There is one, you would say, [that] is a crystal healing temple. It is a necessary place for all to come inspect it and come and see, who can fulfill the greatest task.

Session 23

(Editor's note: the following session was videotaped outside in the backyard.)

Krista and Katherine are the birds.

Krista (Laughing): I'm ready now. You can tell.

Orion Council: Hello, friends.

Katherine: Welcome.

Orion Council: Hello, friends. It's a nice day.

Katherine: Beautiful day.

Orion Council: Well, how are you today?

Katherine: Great.

Orion Council: We are wanting to discuss Ascension.

Katherine: But before we do that, we have some unfinished business.

Orion Council: Yes, well, we certainly want to complete the message.

Katherine: Please.

Orion Council: Eight is the focus of the freedom that is immense within yourself. You do not realize, dear ones, that, when you focus on freedom you are expanding. These are words we use so lightly in this society, but, freedom is your birthright. You came in free and you will leave free.

Katherine: We were talking about the different ways that Orion energies focus.

Orion Council: Yes, okay. Many want to know what is a council? Councils govern galaxies, many councils. We simply exist in one specific frequency when we are speaking of creative energy, life-force energy. We are focusing one specific frequency, you see. We have many focuses in many, many dimensions, but one of these dimensions is quite active at the moment where you are receiving a message, so to speak, from the source of the message — from the frequency, the creative frequency, yes, frequency of creative energies. Creating is what you are supposed to be doing. Yes, creating constantly creating, creating, creating. Many councils exist because creation is organized. Creation is organized. It's frequency of organization — that is what is governing the councils — organization energy. Well, it is fun to be here with so many lightworkers. Yes, when you are free you are what is called a no-man's land. Can you understand? It's friendship energy of no-man's land, energy of no-man's land. It's friendship energy. It's hold on...it's hard to feel this message without containing the light completely. Hard to understand when the energy is so intense. Hard to understand. You all have to feel into the energies. What are you all waiting for? Time to wake up. Time to finish the job. Well done, so far. Time to finish the job.

Katherine: Finish what job?

Orion Council: Anyone ready? You are all watching and waiting but you all watching are the workers of light. You see our point? The promise of God is that you will be taken care of. Can you remember? It is time to remember. All of you must remember who you are. You must walk and remember and walk and remember. It's time.

Katherine: When you say "finish the job," which job?

Orion Council: Well, it is a job of you all. It is the energy that you came in with. The energy you promised Earth. You promised Earth you would help raise the light. You promised. It is time to remember your promise. We want to say that you all are beautiful. You are all so beautiful. You have to help each other more than before, but it is easy now, you have tools. You have to be free and also love each other. It's time to love and be free, in your hearts and your minds, as you understand, dear ones. It's time to forgive —we said this yesterday — it's time to forgive and you can move on. Time to forgive. Why are you all waiting? It's time. Happy squirrels in this backyard. Happy squirrels in this backyard, wanting attention. They want attention, too. Send love to the animals. Can you see them, friends? Can you show the squirrel, friend? On the camera, friend? Can you show them on camera, please.

Katherine: Yes, I did.

Orion Council: It's okay, now. It's afraid. Ha, ha! It is not afraid, it is a creative energy.

Katherine: Well, I just want to note that the squirrel came quite close.

Orion Council: Well, yes, it was wondering, "What is happening in my land?"

Katherine: And as soon as I turned the camera on, it decided to take off.

Orion Council: It was not ready for fame. Okay. Our joke, over now. It's time for us to leave but we have to tell you we love you.

Katherine: Thank you.

Orion Council: We love you. It's time to forgive and to create. Be free in your hearts now, friends. It's time. Goodbye.

Session 24

(Editor's note: the following session was videotaped outside at night.)

Krista: I'm so excited to do this.

Orion Council: Well, hello. How are you, friends?

Katherine: Welcome.

Orion Council: Thank you. Beautiful sky, is it not? We are wanting to discuss Ascension, as usual. When do we not want to discuss Ascension with you? Tonight you are looking at the sky. You are seeing that you have endless opportunities. Imagine you have a space craft and are able to explore the cosmos. Imagine that. Quite a step up from a car.

Katherine: Literally.

Orion Council: Yes. We are wanting to discuss Ascension. In the new paradigm, you will all be traveling quite a lot, you see. You will all be focused on your opportunities. We say, you are completely free and freedom is your birthright. That is our focus today. Freedom is your birthright, you see, friends. When you are focused on the freedom, that is how you free your mind. Your mind, as they say, it is "mind-controlled" — you are all familiar with that. The mind controls your actions, the mind is used as guidance. The mind is used as something to give direction to all of your lives. It is a useful tool to navigate this world, just as a spaceship navigates the cosmos. If you think of your mind as a spaceship, you see, it can go many places.

231

When focused, it is quite interesting, because focused energy can become quite intense and magnified, amplified, when it is focused. You see, when you focus on certain things, you create a better result. A mind or a spaceship that is constantly traveling has no destination. This is why we guide you today, to focus on that which you want, because the opportunities are endless. Just as you would enter a spaceship, you would focus on the destination. You would not focus on every destination all at once; your spaceship would simply fall from the skies. You would be focused on navigating with your spaceship, making sure it was attuned to the right frequencies at all times. We are glad to be here and we would like to discuss Ascension. This is a program that you have all set up, and you are all remembering it is a program.

Many of you are interested in the government and how it is operating. Is it benevolent? Is it not? That is not the priority. Government is there for structure, just as the mind is there for navigation. All of you wanted structure before. Things are changing, of course they will, but we say structure is quite necessary at this time. What is your structure and how are you constructing your realities? What do you need to build a house? A chair needs four legs. A house needs a foundation. Many of you are finding each other because one foundation helps another to spring off of one's self and to become more. Many of you are discovering each other's gifts at this time and we say, it helps in the whole navigating of the space craft. We enjoy these analogies because many of you are wanderers of the cosmos. Yes, Orion here today, and today we are focused on navigating with the mind. The mind is sometimes out of control. This is why you have structure and it is quite useful. Do not dislike your government, do not dislike structure. Only enjoy the fact that you have a stable reality. Physical world has form, it is very structured. We also want to say that you are free. Within a structure you are free and this will seem quite contradictory to many. How can I be free when there is so much structure around me? We guide you in saying that when you remember you are free, you are freeing your mind, you see. It is a question of freeing the mind. You may be able to transcend the body even, when you have freed the mind. However, we say that this is not what you have come to do because many of you lightworkers are here to help. So you came and said, "I would come and be a part of the structure and I would have red hair and I would wear a pink dress and have some black boots." That is the structure you agreed. You said, "I am a multi-dimensional Creator and I want to experience the structure." We say that you must agree with parts of the structure. You do not have to believe all is correct, but we guide you to say, to agree somewhat with the structure at this moment and work with that structure that you are living within, around, in, out, around, so on and so on. Use the structure to create the new paradigm, you see. Use the tools you have to create more light. Use what you have at hand and help each other with each other's gifts and empower the ones around you and you will see the new beginning will be quite wonderful. It has already started and it is quite magnificent. We love you, goodbye.

Session 25

(Editor's note: The following session was videotaped.)

Orion Council: Hello, everyone. Orion Council, here. More in the body than yesterday. How are you all doing? We want to speak of Ascension to all of you watching. Eyes open, now. New changes coming about. Yes, Krista has received quite a download of information. If has been a while since we have been in the body, more so than yesterday. Krista wants to show you all. She has love for new technologies. She wants this in the video. We want to speak of Ascension. We are now more so in the body than before. This is quite exciting. Yes, we had quite a cry. It was lovely to come more so into the body than before. Ah. Eight of us, you ask? We are eight. We are here and we want to help you all at this time. We know who you are, lightworkers, yes, from star systems. You are wondering if we have a spacecraft. We do not need a spacecraft. You are funny humans. You are thinking we are green aliens. We are Orion, Council of Orion. Do you know what is a "council?" Governing the star systems [are] many councils, at this time. We are wanting to discuss Ascension and we feel it is appropriate to say, that at this time, you are all increasing your light quotient. You are all becoming more of who-you-are. You are all beautiful Beings of Light. You are all magnificent Creators. Before Krista channels, she feels like falling asleep; a sign we are coming in to speak. Okay, okay. For those of you wanting to channel, it is possible, however you must be raising your energies through intent. You must raise your energy through intent, first and foremost. What is your intention? If you are wanting to communicate Divinity, you do every waking moment of your life, friends. Do you understand us when we say you are Divinity, you are Beauty, you are Love, you are Light? We are Orion Council and we love you, goodbye.

Session 26

Krista: Whoa, I'm getting this feeling like I'm in water. I was reading Edgar Cayce's work about Atlantis and the Council is coming through. I feel like I'm sinking in water — this blue-green water. Oh, that's what it is, the sinking! I feel like I'm being submerged in water right now.

Katherine: Do you think it really sank?

Krista: Yes. It did sink. It did sink...

Orion Council: Hi. Hello.

Katherine: Hello.

Orion Council: It's nice to be here. We are putting her under the sea.

Katherine: Why?

Orion Council: To experience what is there. She is seeing under the sea — going below water level now. Yes, it is a deep, deep sea.

Krista: They're showing me some kind of sphere. I can't see it, but I'm going deeper and deeper into the water. I could channel, but I could also describe what I'm seeing.

Katherine: Go ahead.

Krista: Okay, so there's this light coming from the sphere and I'm being submerged deeper and deeper into the water. It's bright light and as I'm going into this bright ball of light, and the water's above my head, I'm going into this light. It's underneath the sea. It didn't take long to get there. Okay, I'm in front of this light.

Orion Council: Hello. It is nice to be here. We are from Central Sun.

Krista: Part of my consciousness is still seeing this light, and part of my consciousness is outside of the water — above the water. Somehow, right below me, I can't see this, I can't look into it, it's so bright.

Katherine: How does the light feel to you?

Krista: Gosh, I feel like I'm not in my body from my throat down. My throat is still clear — I'm still able to talk — but I feel them. I feel something in my body from my throat down, now.

Katherine: So do you think they're coming in?

Krista: I don't know. Okay, the light is increasing. Even with my physical eyes, I can see more. My eyes are closed but there is even more light. Yeah, they're in my body, wanting to talk through me but they're allowing me to speak, now there is more light now, all around. There's some layer in between. I can't explain it.

Katherine: What's the feeling of it?

Krista: There's more . . . it's coming over my head, now. This light is like my third eye. Something's being opened or something is changing. I'm getting an interesting sensation in my physical vision. There's all this light. It keeps changing. It's my third eye opening! Oh, great. (Smiling) Okay! I just feel so cool. I just see things! Yes, it's opening, that's what happening. I've been waiting for this for a long time. I feel so good. I feel so nice. Wow, it's like something keeps changing in my vision. They're in me, but it's just like light in my forehead. See, before I had to try hard to do this, but now it's happening spontaneously, which is fun. That's what I like about it. Before, I would feel this discomfort because my eyes would keep rolling back. Okay, now I see, it's open now. It's open. It's bigger now. Before, I would see a circle. Now, it's bigger. It's over my face. I'm getting different sensations in parts of my forehead.

Katherine: Do you feel as if you are still under water?

Krista: No. I feel as if I'm in the room and I feel very clear. I kind of feel hollow.

Katherine: Are you seeing geometries, then?

Krista: Last night I felt the crown open and it usually just twirls in a circle, but now it's making the flower shape, the infinity. It makes four leaves. I feel very peaceful, I don't feel fatigued. Something's holding up my back so that I can sit. It's very comfortable. I feel like I could sit like this all day. It's like a Christed state. Oh, as I say that I feel my crown opening... Beautiful, I feel there's a white light somewhere. I'm seeing in my mind's eye that I'm surrounded by a Christed light.

Katherine: We truly are.

Orion Council: Hello, friends. It's nice to be here. A saintly feeling; it is like being a saint. Can you understand? It is a nice feeling when the crown is open, it allows for the Christed Consciousness to come through. Can you understand? It is so beautiful. We like to feel this with her.

238

Katherine: Are you able to feel it also?

Orion Council: Yes. We have opened the gate to Christ, [pronounced 'krst'] energy. So beautiful. How beautiful.

Katherine: Do you experience that yourselves?

Orion Council: We can, but we know how nice it is when you have not felt it in a long time.

Katherine: Meaning, within a body?

Orion Council: Yes. My, it is nice feeling. Wanted to talk but cannot talk now. It was nice to talk but we cannot talk now . . *Hallo.*

Katherine: Hello.

(Another energy): Angel here.

Katherine: Well, hello!

Angel: Yes, well, it's nice to have fun. Have fun. Having fun. Yes, having fun, now. It's nice.

Katherine: Which angel; White Light?

Angel: Angel of Light, Angel of Light.

Katherine: That's fine.

Angel: How are you?

Katherine: I'm very happy to observe what I'm observing.

Angel: It's nice to see you. You are beautiful, as usual. We love you so much. We love you so much. Can you feel us? Oh, we love you. How we do. Can you feel us?

Katherine: I can now, yes.

Angel: We love you so much.

Katherine: Thank you.

Krista: Mom! A lightning flash went through me! I could go back. Should I go back? Oh my gosh!

Katherine: Your eyes are radiant.

Krista: That felt good. Do you know what I thought? It still feels like I'm in my stomach. I feel like they're still in my body, which is why I'm so excited. It's like something's planting me in this chair — yes, they're going to talk.

Orion Council (Enthusiastically and humorously): Yes. Surprise! Hello.

Katherine: Hello.

Orion Council: We like you.

Katherine: I like you, too!

Orion Council: Hello. It is us. Orion Council, here.

Katherine: I know.

Orion Council: Yes. Hello. How are you today?

Katherine: I am happy to talk with you again.

Orion Council: We are happy to talk with you, as well.

Katherine: Thank you.

Orion Council: Okay. How is it on this Earth plane, now?

Katherine: A lovely day, today.

Orion Council: Is it?

Katherine: It's good to feel physical, today.

Orion Council: We love you. You are beautiful.

Katherine: As I'm sure you are.

Orion Council: Yes. We love you so much. You are so beautiful. My goodness.

Katherine: What color are the lights, now?

Orion Council: The lights? Where?

Katherine: You talk about lights.

Orion Council: In the room? Around us, perhaps? Chakra colors? Aura colors?

Katherine: Bingo!

Orion Council: Angels?

Katherine: Bingo!

Orion Council: Fairies?

Katherine: Are *they* here?

Orion Council: Yes.

Katherine: So, can you speak about —

Orion Council: Unicorns!

Katherine: They're nearby?

Orion Council: As usual.

Katherine: How nice.

Orion Council: One licked your face now, do you like that?

Katherine (Joking): Here is an apple.

Krista: I felt a shudder, here.

Katherine: Maybe Windemere's tail.

(Ed. note: Krista's name for her unicorn.)

Krista: Yes, maybe that was. I felt like a vibratory shudder. I feel an energy between us. Something is right here, pointing to you.

Orion Council (Playfully): It's Windemere, or whomever. Oh, goodness. A horsie In your face. Windemere get out of the way, please. Oh, goodness. Wanting to walk all over you both. Go away. Licking your face.

Krista: I see a huge horse, right now. It doesn't have eyes. Kind of like...I feel strange. I feel like this light beam is open here, like a tunnel. And there's a horse with no eyes. It looks plain, like tan or camel colored.

Katherine: I love that color. Does it have a mane?

Krista: I don't really see the mane it's not really present. I don't see it with or without one, I just see it has a tail. I'm not really aware of its legs. It's etheric. It's like its tail is on me, right here. It's all over you, like it's licking you all over. Maybe that's your old horse [Caesar] because it's like a regular horse, not a unicorn. Maybe it has become a unicorn, I don't know.

Session 27

Orion Council: Well, yes, it was nice entry.

Katherine: Who's entry?

Orion Council: Well, there are few of us here. Wise One. Hi there, hello. He's speedy, he is fast.

(Krista's brother, Kier enters the room.)

Katherine: Yes, he is.

Orion Council: Yes. He is so handsome. Goodness! Look at him.

Katherine: What are some of the colors around his aura just now?

Orion Council: He thinks he is physical, hah! He thinks he is a physical being. And Krista already saw he is orange. Yes. He's got many, but red-orange. He's got lots, but red-orange.

Katherine: Do you have any words for him?

Orion Council: Grounded energy is your energy. Grounded in the physical — this is why we say, he thinks he is physical. He is focused on the physical world. He thinks he is a physical being. He is a light energy in physical form. Good to remind you of who you are, dear one. Hello. Dear one, hello.

Kier: Hello.

Orion Council: Goodness, you are handsome. We, on the Other Side, want to say hello. You are quite handsome in physical form. Well, on with the show. Have a nice night. Merry Christmas. Goodness, it was a pleasure to see him here.

(Kier leaves)

Katherine: Always.

Orion Council: Well, yes. We have come more into the body than before. Hello. We see you, friend. Yes. We see you. Do you understand how we see you?

Katherine: Yes.

Orion Council: Good. Now, it is easy to communicate when we can control the hand movements more so. This was what was happening earlier.

Katherine: You were coming in?

Orion Council: Yes. We were able to move and direct the flow of the hand movements. Well, it does help to control the energy during the discussion. Yes? You are noticing Esther Hicks, yes? Oh, you realize the similarity, yes? My, Krista is good. She has lots of vocabulary. You understand. Easy for us to communicate on the same level. Okay, how are you? We are many, focused in one. Yes. Many of us are wanting to communicate with you. Channel is quite clear at the moment. Easy for us to talk with you right now. Yes. Yes.

Katherine: Is this Orion?

Orion Council: Yes, it is Orion, bright and clear now. Energy very high in the room. Perfect day for channeling. Okay, how are you?

Katherine: All eight, there?

Orion Council: Yes. There are several more. Yes, do you want to know who is in the room in non-physical?

Katherine: Yes.

Orion Council: Everyone. Ha, ha, ha, ha! You do not understand our humor. You think you are physical. You believe you are physical. You are in the room, in non-physical, too.

Katherine: I understand that.

Orion Council: Yes. Funny, how the humans tend to forget they are also non-physical energy. Okay, okay. Quite bright lights she is seeing, now. It is beautiful to have an open crown chakra. How the eyes opening even more. Oh, it is so refreshing to be here with a physical vessel. It's beautiful. You do not understand how beautiful it is to speak with you. Oh, Christed energy here. Oh, it is beautiful energy, here.

Katherine: How does it feel for you to be inside?

Orion Council: It feels so magnificent.

Katherine: To move that left hand and that right hand?

Orion Council: It feels magnificent. We love physicality! Ha ha ha!

Katherine: When was the last time you were in?

Orion Council: We were ages — never! Come on. We do not live physical lives. We are focused in Orion energy.

Katherine: I know that; that's not what I meant.

Orion Council: No, you wanted specific answers: what time? What year? Are we Atlantean? You have these kinds of questions.

Katherine: No, I do not have those kinds of questions.

Orion Council: Oh, what do you want to have answered, then?

Katherine: You said, once before that it's been a long time since you've been in the body and I know that you also said you never were.

Orion Council: We are a humorous bunch of Spirits. Are we not, Wise One?

Katherine: Yes, you are very humorous.

Orion Council (Referring to Kier): He is very busy on the computer, as usual. We do not want to disturb however time is of the essence, so we will continue with the discussion, yes?

Katherine: You seemed to contradict what you said earlier.

Orion Council: Well, you are quite intellectual so we understand where you are coming from. We have not lived physical lifetimes, you see. We are from Central Sun, we live in a different energy focus.

Katherine: Well, I understand all that but I thought you were perhaps talking about another channel [physical vessel], when you said, "It has been a long time since we were in a body."

Orion Council: Our energy is too great to be in one physical vessel. We have incorporated some of our energy in a physical vessel. Do you understand, friend? Some of our energy can be focused in the physical — it is not all of our energy. We are a *vast* energy of Light Beings. We do not need to express all of our energy into one physical vessel. It is only partial. Can you imagine all the light, friend?

Katherine: She would evaporate into light dust, yes.

Orion Council: Perhaps, yes. The heart wants to expand its field. It is comforting, sometimes, because energy is so strong. So much light.

Katherine: Oh, I see. Am I speaking to "Leader" right now?

Orion Council: You are near the truth. Near the truth. Krista is not afraid anymore. It's, yes, time for us to become Oneness. One energy. One energy. Yes. Leader here, yes.

Katherine: Do we have eight?

(Another energy, speaking slowly): Nice . . to . . speak . . with . . you . . Hard . . to . . speak. It is hard to speak.

Katherine: Why?

(Another energy): Have . . not . . practiced . . T-t-t-time . . to forgive. Hard to communicate. Okay, hold on, much light here. Amount is so great — hard to be in the body. Hard to...Hard to... Hard to speak. Archangel...energy.

Katherine: Welcome. Name, please?

(Another energy): Sandalphon.

Katherine: Well, *hello!*

Archangel Sandalphon: H . . H . . Hi. Can we communicate?

Katherine: Welcome.

Archangel Sandalphon: Hi. Can we communicate? Oh, it's so bright. Hello. Archangel Sandalphon, here. Angel Sandalphon, here. Can you forgive others, please? Can you forgive others, please? Energy of forgiveness is now essential. Okay. Message from Sandalphon, okay? I love you.

Katherine: May I ask you a question, please?

Archangel Sandalphon: Yes, quickly.

Katherine: Forgiveness. Talk about forgiveness.

Archangel Sandalphon: Light is strong. When you forgive you will heal so many aspects of yourself. Must leave now.

Katherine: Thank you.

Archangel Sandalphon: Nice to see you. Hold onto those you love dearest. Archangel Sandalphon loves you. Goodbye.

Katherine: Goodbye. Thank you.

Orion Council: My, there are many angels who want to speak with you. Orion here, hello.

Katherine: Hello.

Orion Council: Has been a while, since Sandalphon came through. Can you forgive? Sandalphon wants you to forgive.

Katherine: Yes. It's so important.

Orion Council: So many angels. Hard to contain so much light in one body.

Katherine: Is [Archangel] Michael there?

Orion Council: Maybe. Nice try. Hard to be in one body.

Katherine (Musing): Sandalphon . . .my goodness.

Krista (Krista breathing heavily): I can't do this! So much energy! Oh, it's so much energy, Mom. You don't understand what I'm seeing!

Katherine: No, I don't see what you see.

Krista (Laughing): Oh my God, I feel like I'm going to float. Like I said last time, I feel them. I feel like I'm going to levitate. Oh, there's so much light! Oh my God, oh my

God! I feel like I'm a cloud of light. Oh my God! I can't get over it. I've never felt this way, before. I mean . . .

Orion Council: Hello, friends.

Katherine: Hello.

Orion Council: It is time for us to speak. Energy is so perfect today for channeling. Orion here, hello.

Katherine: Hello.

Orion Council: You see, how when the angel, Krista says, "When angels come in it is slow because energy is so strong?"

Katherine: Yes.

Orion Council: You think we are strong in our light quotient, you do not even realize the extent of the angels' light. Hard to communicate. Angels want to speak, however it is not easy to channel Archangels. They are here, but it is so much light. Your physical vessel cannot hold light quotient — you would simply turn into stardust, as you said. However, they will say hello. As you know, we work with them.

Katherine: Yes. I would like to say hello to some others.

Orion Council: They are trying hard to say hello. You will recognize the different ones. They have different energies. You are noticing the energy differences. Yes?

Katherine: Yes.

Orion Council: Okay. My, it is nice to be here. Orion here, but different focus of energy. You see we have different focuses of energy and different communication styles. Depending on your question, you will receive a different energy response. Understand?

Katherine: Yes.

Orion Council: It is what you are doing, as well. We have our agenda but you have yours. We respect you very much. Okay?

Katherine: Ditto.

Orion Council: Hmm...Yes, you are beginning to see how different we all can be in the non-physical.

Katherine: Yes, how delightful is that!

Orion Council: Nice.

Katherine: Very nice.

Orion Council: How can we be of assistance?

Katherine: Could we speak to Michael?

Orion Council: Well, too hard, some more . . .Krista . . .too much, energy.

Katherine: Just want to say hello to you.

Archangel Michael: You are so beautiful. Can you see yourself? Can you see yourself?

Katherine: Not yet, but I am learning.

251

Archangel Michael (Forcefully): You *must* see how you shine. You *must* see how you are shining. Okay. Look in the mirror. Only one time. Remember who you are. I am Michael. I am Michael. Energy of Sword of Michael. You must remember to free yourself from restraint of others.

Katherine: Help me do that, please.

Archangel Michael: It is done.

Katherine: Thank you.

Archangel Michael: Help... is always...here. When you ask we give our service to you. But you must ask us first. Okay?

Katherine: Yes.

Archangel Michael: Okay?

Katherine: Okay. Question. Are there Michael families? I've heard of people talk of families.

Archangel Michael (Strongly): It is one energy of Michael. You can contain this energy in your field if you request it in your field. It is an energy. You can consider it a family if that is what you are wanting it to be.

Katherine: How do I request that energy in my field, please?

Michael: Well, it is done.

Katherine: Thank you. Thank you for visiting.

Michael: You are most welcome.

Katherine: Goodbye.

Orion Council: Hello. Orion here. Well, you are quite the naughty one, asking all the angels to work for you.

(Laughter)

Orion Council: Can you give them a break?

(Laughter)

Orion Council: Come on! Angels need to rest, too.

Katherine: I think you are —

Orion Council (Interrupting): Just kidding.

Katherine: I thought you were kidding.

Orion Council: Okay. How can we help you?

Katherine: Can you talk about forgiveness, please?

Orion Council: Yes. Forgiveness energy is what is required at this time. Many of you lightworkers are in turmoil, because some do not understand you and the way you behave, the way you do. It is all in Divine Order, you see. You must understand that you are the way-showers for others. Hence, you are happy people and hence, you have well-being in your field. That is because you came to show the way. You came in here with certain abilities. You came in here with specific qualities and you came in here with perceptions others do not have, at the moment. You were born into families that would serve you well, because your purpose was not to suffer. Perhaps you see others suffering. You are not suffering in the same way because you are the way-showers and you all have missions. And you all will fulfill your missions. And you will see that when you show the way, you will always be taken care of, you see. You must trust in the system of, well, Life Itself. The universe takes care of its lightworkers. You do not trust but that is a human response. Okay, you are forgiven and you must forgive others who are not realizing their paths are also sacred and they are taken care of. Everyone has their own challenges, you know, and this is a reminder to you that when you are on your path you will feel bliss. When you are a way-shower, you do not have certain challenges that others have. That is not your focus. You are not required to focus on poverty, for example. A very crude example. We do not enjoy the poverty example because we see you all as abundant however many of you in physical form do focus on socioeconomic levels, as you were discussing before, prior to the channeling.

Katherine: Yes.

Orion Council: You did not come in with those challenges because your lessons were not involving manifesting physical money. It is a different kind of abundance you are all searching, you see. You must remember your mission. That is your task, now. You have been following your mission intuitively. Now you can realize it in your waking state. Many tools are available to you and everyone will be giving pieces to each other. Your abilities are returning to you, the ones you are, well, the innate abilities you have, as spiritual Beings of Light. Humans have come in with certain abilities; have not realized that they have the ability to communicate with the dead. They do not realize they are telepathic and they can see aliens with their third eyes, for example. Many abilities, yes.

Katherine: So you are not just referring to lightworkers, are you?

Orion Council: When you say "lightworker," we know your association with a specific type of human: one of service, one that is love energy. Light. Oneness. One heart. One love.

Katherine: Heh, heh, yes . . .

Orion Council (Singing): Let us, get together, and feel all right.

(Ed. note: The Council sings the refrain from Bob Marley's song, "One Love")

Katherine (Laughing): Oh, the Orion choir!

Orion Council (Singing): One love. Yes. Orion sings, too. Many other tricks.

Katherine: Many other tricks up your sleeve?

Orion Council: Yes.

Katherine: Do you know the energy of Bob Marley?

Orion Council: Well, we recognize energy of Bobby. We called Bobby "angel" before. Do you remember?

Katherine: Yes, I do.

(Ed. note: earlier, the Council had given an example of "Angel Bobby" which may have referred to the photograph of Bob Marley in the room.)

Orion Council: He is an angel, now. Can you understand?

Katherine: Yes. Can we get back, then, to the forgiveness piece — understanding what that really is? You know, from our human perspective, we tend to think of forgiveness as something that we do for or to others. We make the mistake of feeling as if we are coming from this noble place of, "I will forgive you" but I know that that is not true forgiveness.

Orion Council: It is working with the heart center. You must become heart-focused. Energy flowing from the heart feels different from the one in the mind. You have mastered the mind, friend. Okay.

Katherine: When you spoke a moment ago, of "mission," I thought that the mission was the same as the purpose of Ascension — to know who we truly are. Is that correct?

Orion Council: If you continue to beat the drum of who you are, you will not remember your mission because you are stagnant. Your soul wants to experience certain things but do you allow for them to happen —is the question, because you have free will at all times, friend.

Katherine: What is the mission?

Orion Council: To help others appreciate each other.

Katherine: Well, for them to appreciate each other, they have to first appreciate themselves. Is that not so?

Orion Council: Helping bring people together you see, in your work, you have helped many to appreciate one another. Something not quite practiced before. It was a model of perfection that was used before, in many institutions — religious, educational, and so on and so on. You are helping others to relocate and to refocus themselves in a way that is beneficial to the entire group.

Katherine: Can you be more specific, please?

Orion Council: Well, we are giving you an example of what you have been doing with your school.

(Ed. note: Katherine produced a Saturday school program for several years.)

Katherine: Yes, I sensed that, but could you be more specific, please?

Orion Council: We do not give specific answers because a mission is general. You are the creative one, dear one. If you want a mission, there are many energies that will assign you a mission. Have you asked — who is your favorite Ascended Master, perhaps? Which Ray of Creation? Which Archangel? How do you want to complete your mission? Do you want to bring people together in a circle of dance and song? You have done so. Do you want to bring people together for a lesson? You have done so. Do you want to bring people together in love of who they are? You have done so. Dear one, you are doing so well. Do you want to bring three together? You have done so. Do you want to bring thirty or how about a few thousand? You have done so, dear one, it is beautiful what you have done.

Katherine: I don't remember the bringing together of thousands. I would love to remember that.

Orion Council: Do you think that the only energies are physical, at your festival? We are quite offended, friend.

Katherine: Oh, I'm sorry, I do recall the festival.

(Ed. note: Katherine produced a cultural festival for several years.)

Orion Council (Feigning disappointment): Dear one, we are offended, now.

Katherine (Laughing): Oh, no you're not! Yes, thank you for the reminder of the festival.

Orion Council: Well, we hope that you will consider what we have said this evening because you must realize, dear one, that you have been on your mission for quite some time and you are an expert.

Katherine: So, you are saying, that it is simply bringing people together? I think.

Orion Council (Beginning to sing): Yes. You have done quite well. Dear one, we love you and we wish you . . a Merry Christmas, we wish you a Merry Christmas.

Katherine: I'm going to teach you some new songs, okay?

Orion Council: All right. We are ready for any song you want to teach us.

Katherine (Singing and clapping rhythmically): *Funga Alafia, ashé, ashé; Funga Alafia, ashé, ashé* — sing it with me! *Funga Alafia, ashé ashé!* Sing to Orion!

Orion Council: Oh, that was a beautiful song! We love this so much. The angels are screaming. They are dropping their wings, dancing in the room.

(Laughter)

Orion Council: Well, you are quite a joy-giver to all of us. Thank you, dear one.

Katherine: You're welcome.

(Break)

Katherine, Kier and Krista: Kodoish, Kodoish, Kodoish, Adonai Tsebayoth.

Orion Council: Yes, yes, that was beautiful. Yes. Orion, here.

Katherine: Hello, welcome.

Orion Council: We can withstand a prayer, yes.

Katherine (Laughing): Then why is Krista still resisting?

Orion Council: Well, it is as you say: the part that does not like it, is darkness. She does not want to articulate it in that manner, but we call it that because you associate — light and dark, evil and good. You are humans, you associate in that way.

Katherine: Although there is no such thing as both.

Orion Council: Exactly, all is light, all is light. Hello, friends.

Katherine: Hello, hello.

Kier: There is no good, there is no evil? There is only One?

Orion Council: Wise One, well, all is All-That-Is. Yes, it simply "is." No right or wrong. Humans have created right and wrong. Only difference is many layers of being. If you think of it as an onion, perhaps, — no, not quite. Think of it as a multilayered device. One device, what is the device inside you? You are both quite right, however we want to stay with this analogy. It is a round device. What is within the device? Well, the device splits in two. It is still the same device, and those split, and so on, like a cell, multiplying. That is what it is and then part of the cell says, "I am a mitochondrion, this is who I am!" We are saying that you are the device, you are the single cell but you stand and you say, "I am a mitochondrion, that is what I am and nothing else. You are nucleus — I am mitochondrion!"

(Laughter)

Orion Council: Yes, that is how we see all of you and you are quite right, Wise One. Yes, orange, orange energy, he is so much orange energy. He is exuding that orange.

Katherine: Now, what's the difference between the orange and the red, please?

Orion Council: Metatron is orange. Red is . . Archangel . . Zadkiel.

Katherine: Zadkiel?

Orion Council: Yes.

Katherine: Oh!

260

Orion Council: Orion, here. We allowed for interruption, but not again, you see.

Katherine: Yes.

Orion Council: Spirit wants to communicate as well. We were able to show you this, but normally we would not allow for it to happen.

Katherine: You were allowing that for Kier to notice?

Orion Council: Well!

Katherine: Hmm. Not a direct answer. That's quite all right.

Orion Council: Yes, the answer is "yes."

Katherine: Thank you.

Orion Council: We are able to communicate Spirit but Orion, here. Hello.

Katherine: Hello.

Orion Council: It is safe, you are safe energy. You do not have to fear us.

Katherine: You are directing this at Kier?

Orion Council: Perhaps we are.

Katherine: I suspect that you are and I appreciate it.

Orion Council: Okay, "mother hen."

Katherine: That's right; always will be.

Orion Council: That's right.

Katherine: It's important for him to know these things — he's only sixteen.

Orion Council: But he is a mighty Being of Light.

Katherine: He needs to remember that.

Orion Council: He knows.

Katherine: He knows, but consciously?

Orion Council: He knows.

Katherine: Consciously, he must know.

Orion Council: Good job. Well, you are both quite fascinating to us because part of your waking Self knows who you are. You do not simply articulate that knowledge. It's not acceptable in society. You do not see it in the commercials, saying, "I am Light Being, buy my toothpaste!"

(Laughter)

Orion Council: That is not quite normal yet, but we say it will be normal. Perhaps not this time around but it will happen. Everyone will know who they are. We say that in the future. You are limitless Light Beings, you see. There is a future, we see it as well. Oh, it is beautiful: vast lands, lots of sand by the water, many communities by the sand. A bright, turquoise ocean. Many sand castles, you could say. Yes, we are showing one of the possibilities. Like Greece, you would say — similar to Greece, but with more vegetation.

Katherine: Greece — meaning, by the sea?

Orion Council: Yes.

Katherine: Krista had a question about light cities. She is talking about building light cities.

Orion Council: Well, she is wanting to know where Americans will build the light city. Potential exists in many places. We do not want to say you cannot build in one place only, however we hint that there are certain spaces, ready for the construction has begun in a few already. Many in your own state are made of light. They simply do not label themselves "light cities."

Katherine: Are you able to mention some of the cities that are already in the process of being constructed?

Orion Council: Many cities are already sitting in the new energy, but they are not light cities. Light cities [have a] dynamic — it has a construction, it has a blueprint. It has a behavioral pattern, a potential. It fosters certain abilities. It gives way for development of specific outcomes. It's hard to explain...your human terms, limiting...Well it is a...frequency...an energy frequency.

Katherine: Who is speaking now?

Orion Council (Krista breathing heavily): It is Orion. Tired. Hard to communicate. But we will answer any other questions.

Katherine: Well, the —

Orion Council: Hard to communicate.

Katherine: Okay.

(Another energy): Hard to communicate. Adrienne here. Hello. Adrienne here. Want to talk to my son. Is he here?

Katherine: No.

Adrienne: Why is he not here? I want to see him. He needs to talk to his Mom. I want to talk to him. I want to tell him that Adrienne is here. I am in spirit. He does not believe it. I am saying I am here. He does not believe that I'm here.

Katherine: Adrienne...

Adrienne: Yes?

Katherine: Can't you just give him an example —

Adrienne: No, it will not work. He is not open-minded.

Katherine: That means that you have to communicate with him when he's sleeping.

Adrienne: He has to listen. But, all right. Fine, I will try. All right.

Katherine: That is when he is more open and less resistant.

Adrienne: Ask him in the morning, "Has he thought of *maman*?" Ask him in the morning, "Has he thought of *maman*," okay?

Katherine: I will.

Adrienne: Ask him, please. Help me.

Katherine: I will help you, yes.

Adrienne: Thank you, I love you too, but he needs to talk to his *maman*. I am here!

Katherine: All right.

Adrienne: Goodness, he is doing silly things. Come on. Time to talk to *maman*. Okay, thank you so much. So kind woman, you are.

Orion Council: Orion here, hello. Quite open, now, you see. Many want to communicate with you. Are you understanding, friends? Many in the room, as we talked to you before we began, we said there would be many wanting to communicate with you and you have seen there are quite a few.

Orion Council: Well, it is nice to speak with you but we have to explain that when you are not in physical form you are unlimited; when you are unlimited you have many options. At all times, you have options [however] it is part of physical reality [that] you feel as if you have [none]. We want you to know that you have a choice. How do you want to live your life? Can you realize that you have options, always?

Katherine: Yes, we were talking about that earlier. Choices, we were saying.

Orion Council: Yes. We have to help her with a new language of light.

Katherine: Okay.

Orion Council: Have to help her with understanding light language. You do not need to reiterate all the past learnings [as] she thinks. You are both having the need to go from A to Zed in an organized fashion but we say, you do not have to go through A to Zed to have a correct channeling experience. You see, you are ready for new information. We do not have to reiterate. You have come to a certain point in your development where we do not have to reiterate certain things. Humans waste time with proof and "tell me this" and the best option, but we say to "go with the flow." That is the new reality, more going with the flow than before. Want to teach Krista the light language so she can speak it and help with the activations of people. Help activate who they are. Ra Consciousness is the one that is helping to activate the other ones to their true selves.

Katherine: Are you referring to Krista's friend, Ra?

Orion Council: It is called Ra Energy. He is one the "reps."

Katherine: Her friend, Rene?

Orion Council: Yes. A friend. Arcturus. A friend. Arcturus. Yes.

Katherine: She wanted to know about her relationship.

Orion Council: It is a fine match.

Katherine: What kind of match?

Orion Council: Match of Heaven. Not quite. You do not enjoy our joke. It's a match. It's too much info. Pardon our expression. Find...Arcturian...Arcturian...Saying...Saying...

Krista (Struggling): I don't know what's going on.

Katherine: They're just trying to say a word you're not familiar with. Just relax.

(Another energy): Saying . . saying . . saint . . saint . . Germain.

Katherine: Saint Germain! Hello!

Saint Germain: Hard to . . hard to . . ex . .press . . energy.

Katherine: Okay, welcome, welcome.

Saint Germain (Smiling): H...h..hi.

Katherine: Hi, Saint Germain.

Saint Germain: Hi. It's . . so . . beautiful . . You are. So . . do . . what . . you . . want.

Katherine: What we want?

Saint Germain: You have to . . yes . . do . . what you want. Yes . . you can . . *do what you want* . . Okay? Can you understand?

Katherine: Yes, yes, thank you.

Orion Council: It is so nice to have the other ones say hello. So many want to speak with you. We want so badly to help . . Orion, here. Okay?

Katherine: Okay.

Orion Council: Yes. Wanting to help. It's well, a fine match.

Katherine: You said "too much information."

Orion Council It was not right for him to hear.

(Ed. note: Referring to Kier, who had entered the room.)

Katherine: Oh! Thank you for being discreet.

(Another energy, very slow voice): Two . . of . . you, one time. . . Might . . we . . add, you . . are . . alarming . . when you . . are . . both . . in . . the . . room. Both of you are frightening.

Katherine: Frightening? Why?

(Another energy): So much light. The darkness does not like it.

Katherine: Which two are you referring to?

(Another energy): Well, the two of you.

Katherine: Krista and I?

(Another energy): Well, yes. It's okay but, they are not ready for all of the information.

Katherine: Oh, you mean the males in the household?

(Another energy): Yes. Sending them some light, we are.

Katherine: Thank you.

(Another energy): Yes. We are energy healers. New info: Orion does energy healing. Yes. Nice. Nice. Yes. He is nice man. Has nice, nice hands. He can heal. He can heal.

Katherine: He doesn't know that.

(Another energy): Not yet.

Session 29

Krista: (Reading from an online source) "The Twin Flame is the ultimate. There is no need to look further for Source, as this is experienced with one another. The joy at this time, as we have prepared long for this event, is overwhelming — even for the many Ascended Masters awaiting this reunion. You are the same Godspark that came from the loving embrace of the Mother-Father God. It is quite a gift that we are coming into harmony with the one other half of ourselves. There is much disbelief with this event and I can only tell you that it is well worth the wait... (Interrupts reading, saying to Orion, "Come on, guys, chill out.")...as many Ascensions are tied into the reunification with the Twin Flame. After working to reconnect and taking the time every day and night to complete the energy work necessary, your Twin Flame is then known as the Consort. Both your missions are one and the same. The responsibility is held equally by both of you. At this point, you have proven yourself worthy of the title, as together you have both conquered the densities to return as one love, one life, one entity." Isn't that awesome, Mom?

Katherine: This is someone's opinion of what it is?

Krista: Orion's coming. Wow; that's all I can say. I just wanted to share this quotation with people.

Katherine: It sounds very beautiful. I don't know about the Twin Flame. I think that is exceptional and rare in the human experience.

Krista: You think it's rare?

Katherine: I think it's extremely rare. So Krista, are you ready?

Krista: That is so strong when you do that, my ego does not like that at all. Ego hates it.

Katherine: Language of light. Kodoish, Kodoish , Kodoish, Adonai Tsebayoth.

Krista: All right. It's gone.

Katherine: Say it with me.

Both : Kodoish, Kodoish , Kodoish, Adonai Tsebayoth.

Orion Council: Well, it was nice of you to pray. How do you feel? Arcturus is on the mind. It is very powerful energy in her energy field, now. Very much so.

Katherine: Yes, I know. So, you were saying about soulmates — could we go back to that, please?

Orion Council: Soulmates are . . .well, it's not easy to describe soulmates.

Katherine: You have a big smile.

Orion Council: We are laughing because energy is funny today. She thinks about this person because she does not know who he is truly.

Katherine: Who is he, truly?

Orion Council (Teasing): Ha, ha. Ha,ha! Not telling you . . . Do you want to know?

Katherine: Yes.

Orion Council: It is the energy of Orion.

Katherine: I know it's you.

Orion Council: Ha, ha, ha! Well, it is not easy to describe. Heh, heh. It's not easy to describe.

Katherine: Try me.

Orion Council: All right. It's energy of Orion. *He* is Orion energy.

Katherine: He thinks he is Arcturian.

Orion Council: He is that, as well. He is many energies in one "dude."

(Laughter)

Katherine: Can we bring him here?

Orion Council: Yes. He is here, now.

Katherine: Can he say something?

Orion Council: He is wanting to ask permission to talk.

Katherine: Yes, it's granted.

Arcturus Ra (In non-physical): Well, hi.

Katherine: Hello.

Arcturus Ra: I am Arcturus Ra.

Katherine: Also known as Rene?

Arcturus Ra: Yes. I have come to propose a toast.

Katherine: Propose a toast?

Arcturus Ra: Propose a toast. I want to organize spaceships. Krista can help. I want to organize spacecraft.

Katherine: For what purpose?

Arcturus Ra: For a free land: to free the people on the land. It will help to facilitate the new learning program. The ships will arrange the energies on the planet Earth.

Katherine: What of light cities? I thought that was your focus.

Arcturus Ra: Yes. I want to create them on Earth. I want to create cities of light. Yes. I want to do that as well. I have to ask for help. I do not like asking for help however, I want to help.

Katherine: I understand, well, thank you for your visit.

Arcturus Ra: I am watching her development. It is important at this time.

Katherine: Yes, I agree with that.

Arcturus Ra: I am overseeing many Ascensions at once. Helping to run the show, in a way. I am benevolent. I am benevolent. I have pure intentions.

Katherine: I am glad to hear that.

Arcturus Ra: I do, I certainly do.

Katherine: Well, thank you. We would like to speak to Orion again.

Arcturus Ra: Do you have any questions for me? Are you worried that I will interfere with your channeling? It is not my intention to interfere. I simply want to guide and assist Krista. She is a kind soul. She can use my help. She can be helped. I want to propose a toast to the Ascension of both of you.

Katherine: Well, let us raise our glasses, not just to the two of us, but to Gaia and all.

Arcturus Ra: Yes. Let us raise our glasses and say thanks to a new world. Arcturian technology will help in this new paradigm shift. Arcturian lightships are already in Sedona. Want to tell you that and that there are many who are aware of the ships. I am commander of a ship and I am here to help people raise their conscious vibes to become more conscious of their true Selves, activating others. I came in today because I want to establish a trust between you.

Katherine: Between whom?

Arcturus Ra: She does not always trust me. She does not always trust me because she has noticed many untrustworthy people in her life but I want to tell you that I am trustworthy.

Katherine: Well, as you know, from our perspective, it's a question of seeing that through what you do, not just what you say.

Arcturus Ra: That's correct. I want to help. Please understand I only have so much or so little to give in this physical world. I want to assist and I want to say that I can be trusted. All right?

Katherine: All right. Krista will hear this later on in the recording.

Arcturus Ra: Nice to communicate this way. I put in some effort.

Katherine: Thank you.

Arcturus Ra: You are welcome. Thank you, ladies. It was a pleasure. Goodbye.

Katherine: Goodbye.

Orion Council: He wanted to come through.

Katherine: So, was that an aspect of him?

Orion Council: That was part of his Higher Self, but not quite. It was his astral body combined with energy from the Higher Self.

Katherine: This is the first time, I think, that we have experienced someone [coming through] who is still incarnated.

Orion Council: Isn't that interesting? It is possible and there are many who witness this in different ways. Hello, friends. How can we help, today?

Katherine: You were speaking of soulmates today.

Orion Council: Soulmates are simply the same spark. They are of the same spark, since the very beginning.

Katherine: Is there a difference between Twin Flames or are you referring to Twin Flames?

Orion Council: Soulmates are like Twin Flames, but not quite.

Krista: I feel exhausted. I wish I could just go out and let them talk. I wish they could just do all the work and I could just lay here and not do anything. All right guys, you've got thirty-five minutes and then I'm coming back in. That's it.

Orion Council: Hello, it's nice to talk but much energy is needed for us to come in. We want to discuss Ascension.

Katherine: We would like to hear you discuss Ascension but we'd like to have this small matter of definitions —

Orion Council: All right, we will clarify. Soulmates contain the same vibration. Soulmates are like siblings, from the same family. Soulmates have a similar mission and task. Soulmates are here to rekindle the Ascension program. To help facilitate Ascension, you need your soulmates. You live a similar life purpose. Soulmates come in groups, representing group energies. Soulmates are free-minded. When they meet each other they are free, because they see their own reflection reflecting back at them and they feel free and they release who they are not. Ra Arcturus would like to speak again.

Katherine: Well, he will have to wait just a moment, because we need to get this clarification straight.

Orion Council: All right. We enjoy the fact that you are taking control of the situation. Krista enjoys that. She feels safe with you.

Katherine: Yes. So the difference, or the distinction between soulmate and Twin Flame is what?

Orion Council: Soulmates carry a similar vibration. Twin Flames complement each other.

Katherine: Complement, as in complementary opposites?

Orion Council: Perhaps you would see it as so.

Katherine: I see. My understanding — correct me if I'm wrong, is that it is very rare, unusual for Twin Flames to incarnate at the same time on same planet and to be partners.

Orion Council: Rare for whom? Come on, who are you? Are you normal?

Katherine: Oh, what is normal?

Orion Council: Twin Flames — who is it unusual for? All in human form? No one in human form can re-unite?

Katherine: Well, that is what I was told and I'm asking if that is accurate or if that's inaccurate. It seems as if you're saying that is not.

Orion Council: You humans are wonderful. You do not understand you are Creators. You will not enjoy our answer, because we will tell you that you create your reality. This you agree with, but many are wanting rules. Many are wanting to play a game. Find the soulmate game, find the Twin Flame game. If you want to create a Twin Flame you can do so.

Katherine: Well, I think that's wonderful news. That's very liberating.

Orion Council: Is it not?

Katherine: Indeed, it is!

Orion Council: Why should it be unreachable? Why should you feel you were left alone on this planet?

Katherine: This is extraordinary news, thank you.

Orion Council: Arcturus Ra would like to communicate.

Katherine: Just a moment; I have a few more questions concerning soulmates. You said that there are soulmate groups?

Orion Council: Soulmates come in groups.

Katherine: So, soulmates do not necessarily mean male-female, as in a partnership.

Orion Council: It is romanticized. Many in the same family are soulmates. Same soul family. Soul family.

Katherine: I get it, excellent information. Thank you. I know you wanted to speak of Ascension.

Orion Council: But do you believe that you can belong to many families, since you have lived many lifetimes in many different galaxies, even?

Katherine: Yes, yes, indeed. It makes total sense.

Orion Council: If you were to marry someone from a different soul family, would you not become their soul family as well? Intermarriage has happened throughout the ages. Many of you humans are a result of intermarriage.

Katherine: Yes. I am very appreciative of your clarification, it was very helpful. We humans keep dodging the *you-are-a-Creator* message and yet ultimately, that is what will set us free from illusion. The reminder is always welcome. I do have another question, though, about the healing process of the angels.

Orion Council: The angels are an added bonus to the healing practice. For sessions, they [the clients] are receiving healing from the angels. We did not tell you this before. We thought it was obvious.

Katherine: When the session is recorded and the clients replay it, are the energetics embedded in the recording?

Orion Council: You can pick up on the energies. You can read the energies.

Katherine: But I mean, specifically on the recordings, such as on our recordings now.

Orion Council: The intention was not to heal [clients] through [these] recordings. If you were to set the intention that a recording would give healing energy, then it will.

Katherine: Who sets the intention?

Orion Council: The client is asking for much needed energy and so they receive much needed energy, because the session is a pure act of service to the other one.

Katherine: Therefore, on the recording that they have, the energies will be embedded? So, when they play it again, a month later, they will receive the benefit thereof? Is that correct?

Orion Council: They will remember that energy.

Katherine: Okay. So when they "remember the energy" they can re-experience it, is that correct?

Orion Council: Yes.

Katherine: So the power always seems to come back to us, individually?

Orion Council: Yes, that is correct.

Katherine: Krista is drawing Reiki symbols in her hand and placing it on her thigh area. I think she needs healing in that area. What do you have to say about that?

Orion Council: The angels are helping, now.

Katherine: Why isn't it an instantaneous process? Why isn't it healed instantaneously?

Orion Council: Because your thoughts dwell upon the pain. If you could change them, immediately, then the healing would happen. You would bring back the reality many times back. Your focus is what changes things.

Katherine: Ah, yes. It goes both ways, then. As the focus moves [changes], so does the situation, correct?

Orion Council: That is correct.

Session 30

Krista: What are we going to ask? I can feel the direction of the energy current.

Katherine: Do you want to pray?

Orion Council: Hello.

Katherine: Hello.

Orion Council: Hello. Yes. Please do pray.

Katherine: Kodoish, Kodoish, Kodoish, Adonai Tsebayoth.

Orion Council: Source, yes. "Source, yes," she [Krista] says.

Katherine: What does it mean when someone says they have "petitioned" Source?

Orion Council: Ask Source permission.

Katherine: I don't understand.

Orion Council: But you know the answer yourself.

Katherine: I know that there is no separation, but it seems there is [when asking].

Orion Council: It seems so because you are physical, friend. You know the truth. You are physical, but you know the truth.

Katherine: If I were nonphysical, I would "go" to Source and petition for a dispensation? It just sounds a little contradictory. I was wondering if you could shed a little light on that for me. My human mind, my rational mind, cannot really grasp that.

Krista: I feel this extreme fatigue. I feel this weird energy, it's like a big triangle pointing down on me. Or like an upside down pyramid. It's not a triangle, it's elongated, geometric. I just see a pyramid with you. I don't know if you're focusing on a pyramid. Do you know what a starseed is, Mom?

Katherine: Yes.

Krista: Yes, I am [one]. I'm just starting to believe it.

Katherine: Yes, you definitely are.

Krista: Heh, heh. I think you may be one of these "crystal adults."

Katherine: Is there such a thing?

Orion Council: It is nice to be here.

Katherine: Welcome.

Krista: Oh, I really feel it in that thigh area. It's really strong.

Katherine: Healing, perhaps.

Krista: It's moving in my leg.

Katherine: Try to relax, Krista.

Orion Council: Yes. Well done. Relaxed is correct way to channel. Hard to relax when the mind can focus in so many ways. It is what helps, but what hinders as well. We are showing her a temple now, inside a temple. Mayan pyramid. Inside a Mayan pyramid, yes, temple. Wanting her to see inside of a temple. There are many doorways.

Katherine: Were these ways to communicate with other systems?

Orion Council: That is the point. Well done, friend, you are intuiting. Okay. Good job. Relaxed helps the channel come through. Well done. Learning to relax.

Katherine: Good, Krista.

Orion Council: Showing the pyramid. Oh, it is nice to be here. We can speak now with a more relaxed mind. Easier to speak when the mind is relaxed. Now, consciously relaxing is helping us very much. We want to talk and talk and talk as we come through. We want to talk and talk and talk and talk and talk.

Katherine: Welcome, welcome, welcome, welcome, welcome!

Orion Council: Yes, well done. We are good, we are good, good, here, yes, yes, yes, yes, okay, okay.

Katherine: All eight of you?

Orion Council: Many of us in the room. There are 12 of us here. Ah, some in the body, some not in the body. Five in the body at the moment. Can you understand? Six in the body, six in the body. You can have them in the body too, if you'd like.

Katherine: Me?!

Orion Council: Yes. Would you like us to come in?

Katherine (Hesitating): I'm not sure.

Orion Council: Well, you can try, but do not have to.

Katherine: Well, I didn't think that I have such an ability.

Orion Council: We can do it together. If you want.

Katherine: When? Wouldn't I have to learn how to relax and so on?

Orion Council: It is all right. We are trying, now. Yes, well done, well done, well done.

Katherine: What's well done?

Orion Council: Well done, well done. Learning to focus. Yes, it is good to be here. Oh, it is so nice to be here.

Katherine: Is the training officer here today, with you?

Orion Council: Yes, it is nice to speak with you today. Yes, training is happening. Well done, well done. Learning to channel comfortably, yes. Yes. Yes. We have been working with her today, yes. Had a little difficulty today with us.

Katherine: Why is that?

Orion Council: Not giving us attention.

Katherine: Can you open your eyes? No?

Orion Council: Has to focus. Has to focus.

Katherine: Krista?

Orion Council: Yes. Seeing so many things at once. We are here. We are Orion Council. Hello.

Katherine: Hello.

Orion Council: We are here to discuss Ascension. It is time now to forgive the past. Forgive — lesson arrives for forgiveness of the Self. Do you see? "One today," Krista says, "one lesson today: how to forgive the Self. I made a mistake, I forgive myself." Do you do it? Do you truly forgive yourself or do you beat up on yourselves?

Katherine: We tend to beat up but we know better.

Orion Council: "We have been taught it is just, it is correct, it is even sovereign to beat up on yourself." Unconscious beliefs formed around degrading the Self.

Katherine (Murmuring): Poor, darling Self.

Orion Council: Free is, free...Krista says health question you want to ask. She says, "Come on, Mom."

Katherine: Okay. Is this something I should be worried about?

Orion Council: Are you creating an issue by discussing it? What will you think about? Health?

Katherine: I choose to think about health and well-being.

Orion Council: Well, now you have lesson. "Oops, I ate the chips." Forgive the Self. Forgive the diagnosis. Forgive them all. Who are you?

Katherine: A Magnificent Being of Light.

Orion Council: Who are you truly?

Katherine: I am Source in expression.

Orion Council: Ah. Do you heal from colds?

Katherine: There is no such thing.

Orion Council: We are not in school. You can answer as you believe it to be true. You do not get points or deducted points.

Katherine (Laughing): Well, we already discussed healing.

Orion Council: Do you recover from colds?

Katherine: Yes.

Orion Council: But you still get them. You have not mastered physical realm, exactly. You would not have these colds.

Katherine: I very, very rarely get a cold.

Orion Council: Well, you have done quite well. So, we do give you grade *A+*.

Katherine: Thank you, and I will give you an apple, an apple to the teacher: joke.

Orion Council (Seriously): It is a funny joke.

Katherine: But you are not laughing.

We are Orion Council. We do not laugh, ever. Ha, ha, ha! *A-*.

Katherine (Humorously): Points off for laughter.

Orion Council: Yes well, it's all right.

Katherine: Thank you for the reminder that it's a question of focus –whether on health and well-being, or focusing on illness and illusion.

Orion Council: Health and well-being, please.

Katherine: Yes, more of that.

Orion Council: You know what you prefer.

Katherine: Yes. You were speaking of Ascension and a time for forgiveness.

Orion Council: Yes, we want to speak of Ascension. Perhaps we will suggest topics for further discussions. Training others to see clearly — who they are. Origin, yes? Krista asks, "planetary origin?" Ha, ha. So proper. "Are you starseed, basically?" She wants to ask as a topic: how to tell if you are starseed.

Katherine: Well, is there anything other than a starseed? If you're not a starseed, what are you, an "Earth soul?"

Orion Council: Many options.

Katherine: Can you name two others for me, please? Just out of curiosity.

Orion Council (Joking): "International angel."

Katherine (Laughing): International angel!

Orion Council: Do you like that one?

Katherine: Yes.

Orion Council: You are international angel. You fly, no?

Katherine: Surely.

Orion Council: What do you prefer?

Katherine: Well, I am an "Earth angel."

Orion Council: Well, do you like that title?

Katherine: No, not particularly.

Orion Council: Well, what do you like?

Katherine: I was interested in hearing that we have starseeds, we have "international angels," angels and human-angels, and what else? It must be vast.

Orion Council: So many names for energy.

Katherine: Yes, for energy. It's all energy. Thank you for that reminder. But you know, that's how we are focused and that's how we will be able to communicate with other human beings, using names and labels.

Orion Council: Yes.

Session 31

(Editor's note: Krista and Katherine have been discussing Krista's recurrent fatigue. She considered discontinuing to channel altogether.)

Orion Council: Well, it is not easy to raise the frequency at all times.

Katherine: Welcome, Orion Council.

Orion Council: Thank you. It is not easy to raise your frequency.

Katherine: And that's what's needed to channel?

(Another energy, in a firm tone): Ask more important questions.

Katherine: What about the DNA?

(Another energy): It is arranged.

Katherine: The new strands?

(Another energy): Will be arranged. New structure will be arranged.

Katherine: Is it happening now?

(Another energy): Yes, of course. You know it. Are you feeling it? Are you feeling the new structure within yourself? So many issues now, you have, with the body; the functions. Not the same as before. Freeing the mind, now. Entering the mind, freedom of the mind is to enter, incorporate the new Self into the free mind. Free your mind and the new Self will be incorporated into it. Free the mind. Great job.

Katherine: That sounds fantastic.

(Another energy): Everyone is waiting for you to free your minds. Free your minds. Free the mind first, then you will experience Ascension. Ha, ha, ha. Hello, friends.

Katherine: Hello.

(Another energy enters): Nice to have you here. Introduction with Archangel . . . .

Krista (Frustrated): I can't say it!

Katherine: Gently, gently . . . .

(Another energy): Emerald, energy. Archangel of Emerald Light.

Katherine: Which one is that?

Archangel of Emerald Light: Nice try.

Katherine (Joking): "But no cigars."

Archangel of Emerald Light: Angel of Emerald Light. Angel of Areon. Have to organize sessions. Have to hold them. Have to organize sessions.

Katherine: Our sessions or group sessions?

Archangel of Emerald Light: Both. Angels, angels want to help . . .organize . . .sessions. Angels want to help. Free the mind, first.

Katherine: Are there steps?

Archangel of Emerald Light: Hold on. You are impatient.

Katherine: Yes, I am.

Archangel of Emerald Light: Come on. It's not easy for us to talk, here.

Katherine: Take your time.

(Another energy enters): Angels, angels, here.

Katherine: Welcome.

Angels: Hi. Organize sessions, please. Organize sessions.

Katherine: Can you be more explicit?

Angels: Well, it's two people at the same time. Two will be involved. Two will be the session. Hard to explain. Have to awaken them. Have to awaken them. It must be done.

Katherine: Two other people other than Krista and I?

Angels: No. Two at a time. One on one.

Katherine: One-on-one session with you?

Angels: No. With the Orion energy.

Katherine: Oh, Krista's *clients*!

Angels: Yes. Well done.

Katherine: Well, thank you. Now I understand what you mean.

Angels: Do apologize . . .do apologize.

Katherine: Not necessary.

Angels: Not necessary. To apologize.

Katherine: No.

Angels: It's okay.

Katherine: Yes.

Angels: Hard to talk with the humans. [Much] energy talking to humans [is required].

Katherine: Thank you for making the effort.

Angels: Free the mind, so you can experience Ascension. It's time.

Katherine: Are there specific, helpful steps in freeing the mind?

Angels: No, you just do it. Easy. Let go of the energy in the head. Release. You have to awaken the heart center. Let go of limiting beliefs. Leave out that which does not work anymore. Only good thoughts. Do it, just do it. You can do it. Just try. Try, friend. Will work out when you just try. Don't "wishy wash" around. Water does not have will, it simply flows. You need to have will-power, will-power to try, not like water. Have will-power.

Katherine: I understand.

Angels: Will. Do not "wish-wash." Have will-power.

Katherine: So you are saying, with intention, yes?

Angels: Yes, do it. First, do it. See for yourself. Energy of Angel of Orion training her. Angels want to train her. It's not easy.

PART II: ANSWERS

Orion Council, here. We are the Orion Council and we are your friends. We are telling you that you are most important in this world at this time because you have a specific energy imprint. Your imprinted energy is what is calling in the angels and we are saying that more of you are needed in this world because you have a specific life of purpose on this planet. You have come in with the gift to help others reawaken those dormant qualities within themselves. When you are discussing these potentials with other people, they are feeling their own mastery. When you are doing this, the other one realizes their connection on an energetic level. We would like to tell you that when you are focused on your connection to the Divine Energies, you are manifesting more Source Energy onto this planet. This planet is healing from the past hurts from the time periods when people did not respect Gaia and we are asking all to respect Gaia with their focus. So, when you have time, would you please send healing energy to Gaia with your meditations? You can do this. It is simple, but many are not focused on the nature of the planet. This is our "agenda" as the Keeper [Krista] calls it, but we are simply wanting the best for everyone. How can we help you?

ON CONNECTION

Well, you ask us if you are from Orion. We have been communicating with you lately and that is perhaps why you are feeling this, quite strong of a connection with us. What does it mean to be "from" a planet? What do you think it means to be "from" Orion? Do you know that it is a star system and there are many, many stars in a system? So how can you simply be from one place only, when you are an unlimited being? Well, we understand that the human mind has a certain capacity to understand our communication. We are trying to speak to you from another level of existence — a multi-dimensional level, you see. Are you from Orion? Well, let us see, your soul has many components and your soul aspects are quite loud, you see. They are wanting to express themselves in this physical plane. This physical plane only holds the capacity for a certain number of your aspects: not all of your aspects can come through at this time, you see. They want to, but they cannot. When you are asking if you are from Orion, we are telling you that many, many, many of your aspects reside there, in this moment, right now. Your energy imprint is quite strong, friend. You have an ability to focus much healing energy on the [planetary energy] grids. The grid has been set up and you are able to fine-tune many parts of [it]. This program has been set up because many humans were not awake. Many humans were needing this new grid because they had to be forced out of bed, to wake up. New grid now is here and many like yourselves are angels, working with us. You are angel of love, you are. You have come to experience life in a physical form because angels are not physical. It is funny how you send us your energy imprint. We know who you are. So funny you are, to tell us who you are. We see you beyond your human cape. You are [an] angel of light. Angel of light, of light, of light.

A MESSAGE FROM ANDROMEDANS

We are wanting to communicate the Andromedan experience. When we communicate with the Earthlings, the Earthlings are surprised at our existence sometimes, because we are so neighborly. We are quite close to them but they are not quite aware of us. We have brought our ships in quite a long time ago but, you see, many are afraid. This is why we cannot reveal ourselves. [We are] with you and want you to know that [we are] focusing [our] light on you every day. When you want to communicate, you can do so through your meditation. All right? So, when you are focusing your intent and your desire to communicate with us, you only need to quiet your mind and we will drop in information to your mind. It will sound like your imagination, but it is us. We are quite close to you.

ON ENERGY HEALING

Many humans have experienced quite difficult lives in the past but they are now ready to heal these hurts. Many are still holding on. It is quite interesting why they hold on to these pains, but so many [others] are healing and wanting to heal but they are not doing it. There is a difference between healing and wanting to heal and wanting to be healed. It is quite fascinating how human beings can be so limited in their thinking of what healing is and how it happens. Energy is always the cause of illness: energy [that] is not released. Regressive Therapy will help you remember. You will see why you have these problems. [You are] having to heal with the mother issues. [You are] forgiving now but still needing to heal mother issues. Not easy when you are feeling you are being walked all over by a mother figure. Not wanting to give up [your] seniority to others. Needing to realize that you can assert yourself, hence, the disorders, irritations and so on. Who is the one to walk over you? No one, dear one: you are a powerful Creator. Do you realize, friend, that when we are channeled, you are being helped on the physical level? We are guiding you now to release and to forgive others.

ON ANGELS

We say that you are always loved, no matter what choice you make. Perhaps you want to vibrate on the Orion Council vibration. Orion Council vibration is creating with love energy. Love energy is from the Godhead but it is expressed differently on your physical plane. Orion Council is focusing on your speaking qualities. When you are speaking to an audience of several people, you will be able to direct this love energy through your speech — not the words you say, but the way you say those words. When you are in an audience, the audience does not focus on the angels in the room. The audience does not focus on their own angels. "Why does Orion always talk about angels," Krista asks. Why, all the time angels? Because not enough people talk about angels. When you are speaking to a group of people, you have an angelic quality about you. So, when you are speaking, you can channel this angelic energy to your audience. How does that feel, dear one? How does it feel to know that your voice channels angelic energy? Does it make any sense at all, Orion asks? When you realize you have this ability, you become an even more powerful lightworker. When you focus this light — this is what we mean, when we say "focus this light" it means, that when your waking self holds this understanding, that the light you have is healing or calming, it is actually doing this, because you are focusing on it. There is so much a human can focus on at one interval. At one time, a human can focus on so many things: " What happened to my laundry yesterday?" "What movie am I going to see tomorrow?" All of this happens when the human is in the moment. Human has so much ability to focus on so many things, but we say, when you come in, before you walk into a situation, to focus the light within. Do not worry, because in the future, you will have more angel stories [from] more people. It is the evolution of the species now, to focus more on the Other Side, to discuss it more. And when it is discussed, the scientists as well will feel more at ease to discuss. How about a scientist who has an angel experience? How would that feel, when ten scientists say they had an angel story to share? They try to experiment and explain. What if a little one says that you are an angel? Who listens to them? You can, perhaps, remember that you are doing lightwork, and you will feel better about the exchange of energy. Many of us, here, are enjoying the unfolding process of the human beings. So many, now, are awake to the possibilities they have in their everyday lives. The possibilities, now, are more so than before, because you are tapping into other levels of existence. We tell you that not everything is revealed because your focus would shift too much. If everyone were to see angels tomorrow, they would not work tomorrow. If everyone were to "wake up" tomorrow, the banks would stop working, the systems would stop working overnight. We cannot let this happen. It is too uncomfortable for human beings. However, because you are awake to the probabilities of the new world, which has, by the way, begun, then, you will understand the potential because you are able to create with the other levels of existence. Do you know about the fairies? Little angel fairies? They [are] making music. The plant kingdom makes music and you can hear angel music if you want to. Krista has heard the angels singing. Everyone can hear, everyone can see, but not everyone is ready for this to happen, because it would be too uncomfortable. This is why we need a gentle soul like yourself, an old soul, who knows everything will be okay, to show the way. We need old, gentle souls to bring in the new energy. We do not want the other ones to feel uncomfortable. We want it to be in the highest good for all.

ON ENERGY TOOLS

When you are creating these [orgone energy] devices, you must focus your energy on the love. We know that is quite a cliché but it is most important because that is what will help you guide your work. When you are not feeling the love connection, you will know you are not connected and you will know that you are not downloading the information you need on another level. So, you must remember to focus your energy on serving, on serving, yes? How are you wanting to develop these tele-communications? What is wrong about the communication devices you are having now? Do you not like the telephone? This is alien technology. Are you quite ready? Ha, ha! We are quite impressed with you. One of us here [is] wanting to discuss the specifics of the technology with you, and we are saying, you must handle these electronics with caution and take caution when you are disconnecting from the device. All right? You must take caution when you are disconnecting because you are elevating to another frequency of communication and when these frequencies are coming through, you will start to connect and you may forget yourself in this work. So, you must remember to disconnect when you are focused on the physical plane. Many of us at this time, are wanting to communicate with you through these devices and when you are tampering with the frequencies, you are often playing with these subtle levels of existence. There are many, many, many different beings on all levels and when you connect with them through one of these devices, you must take caution. We are saying this because we know this is a desire of humans to want to raise the vibration of the planet, so much now that you are willing to quantum leap ahead in your development, but we need the masses to awaken and it is not something overnight, you see. So, when you are focusing on these new developments, you must remember that the masses are not quite awake yet. [To] the few who are willing to accept your technologies, when you are giving to them with the love, you will be raising their frequencies.

ON KARMA

You are wanting to know if you are still having karma. What a timely question. This is a perfect question for many. Hopefully you will share these answers with those you love dearly. Now, what about the karma? Well, the Karmic board — many call them — the channel [Krista]wants to use the term "board." It is not a board, it is a council "karmic council" so to speak. They are deliberating, constantly. They are sipping their coffees and wondering who goes to hell. Ha, ha, ha! Do you like our humor? It is not funny. We are joking, we are joking, we are joking. Karmic board does not exist, anymore. Karmic board is *kaput!* Karmic board is done, karmic board is gone, bye-bye, see you later, *sayonara*. Why so many are wondering about the karma? Oh so many stories about the karmic experience and the punishment and purgatories that have been created by human concepts and experience. There is no such thing as a purgatory. There has never been and there never will be, you see, because you are children of God. Why would God want such a horrible place for His children? It is not possible. Only the human can create such a place because of the dual system that exists on your planet. It is a way to control the minds of many dear lightworkers, who are hoping to elevate the energies, but they are still fearful of the fact that some lightning from the sky will strike them down because they forgot to pay back five dollars. Can you imagine such instant karma? Well, when you are asking about karma, we think you are asking about the fact of "what goes around, comes around." You know, the saying, yes? It is not exactly karma that you ask of, but we understand your question. It is a quite valid question. Yes, the karma is no longer in existence but you have the old belief system of karma still implanted in your minds. It is still a program. It is quite complex when you have ingrained a belief into your mind. It is like a data chip that is not useful but it is still there and the entire system is connected to it. So, you must create something else in place of this "chip" that is malfunctioning. You can still run the old program but it has bugs, you see.

ON SOUL ASPECTS

You are focusing your light in many [unknown] ways. The aspects are being healed because they need to experience a healing and it is not quite just a "hands on" healing, it is on an energetic level. The energies are perfect for your experience, you see. So, if you are asking what needs to be done next, we tell you that when you are focusing [your] light on something, it allows that thing to develop into its highest potential — "highest" for the Earth plane. As a child, you may have felt discordance with many parts of your environment as many parts did not serve those aspects that were wanting to be healed. When you came in, you knew that you would experience these difficulties, however those aspects are quite selfish sometimes and they can get out of control, you see. We will give you an example. When you are a musician who is wanting to fine-tune his instrument, you have a musician who is wanting to create a symphony, as well. So, there is a discord between [one] part of the musician who is the fixer of the instrument [whose] aspect is being satisfied by the fine-tuning of the instrument. The aspect that is the composer [however] is not quite satisfied, because the composer is wanting to compose. Do you understand our example?

The aspect that is wanting to be expressed the most, is the heart, which is the Higher Self. The Higher Self is wanting to "reach down," in your terms. It is wanting to "reach down," which is a task of many humans. It is a step ahead of where you are now, but that is something that is coming next. We are giving you a taste of what is in your potential future and that is a stronger connection with the Higher Self that knows all limits and all boundaries. It can see beyond the Earth plane. So, when you are connected to the Higher Self, you are connected to other galaxies. You are looking into other dimensions. You are looking into other perceptions. You are looking into the experience of others, as well. It is like an all-seeing lighthouse and you are swimming in an ocean of energies that are confronting you and confusing you at times, but it is all for the Highest Good. When you go into your lighthouse, all lights are clear: you are shining a light on the ocean. So, if you are wanting to know what you should deliberately focus on, we tell you, you are on the absolutely right path that is correct for you at this moment. You must remember however, that to focus your light is to do an act of service to yourself, to your Higher Self. So, what is it you are wanting to shine your light upon?

ON MONEY THROUGH SERVICE

The money flows in when you are focused on the abundance aspect of your work. What is it that gives you a feeling of gratitude and what is it that gives you a feeling of contentment? Sometimes the job is second nature. Those jobs are often the ones that are bringing in the "cash" and when you are focusing on the abundance aspect of your work, that is what will bring it in. Are you focusing on an abundance of cash flow? Are you wanting to make more money with your work? Yes. So when you are a success story, the other ones are more inclined to work with you? That is a way that your society is working. The one that holds up the flag and says, "me, me!" is the one whom everyone looks up to. It is not wrong to hold up your flag and to wave it around for others to see. That is quite good. We want to remind you of the integrity, [for] that is what you have done before. That is what has gotten these clients to you. When you are focused on the integrity of assistance, we tell you, it comes back to you magnified. When you are giving with an open heart, that is what the others are feeling and sensing on another level. When you are focusing on this act of service, this "how may I help you" is most important. That is what the people are, psychically you may say, perceiving. When you are coming from a place of "I want to help you, dear one" that is what the people are wanting to hear and they will pay you big money, when you are really, really, really wanting to help them. We ask that you place yourself in this vibration of complete service. When you are writing your text and your self-promotional speeches, you must have that energy of true service. If it is feeling heavy, you will be putting in that heavy vibration into your work. This is why we come to you with this spiritual perspective, that is: you must focus the energy of service.

You are wondering, "what is going on in this channel? Why are those Orions so unusual?" Yes? Well, friend, we are many in this room. Angels wanting to talk with you but are you available for angels to call you? You have heart of gold, you have. Angels saying that you are a nice man. You have the attention span of a kid sometimes, but you can definitely focus your energies. Angels are joking with you. They want you to remember who they are. Angels are wanting you to have a happy lifetime. Angels are saying, you have this transition period now and it will continue into the future but can you focus your energies on your own healing and remember your gift is to help them awaken their own gifts? Angel Tryon...Angel Tryon...energy of Tryon, here. Tryon here. Yes, it's nice to talk with you. Hello. You are this time around making up for other past mistakes. You have healed many parts of your soul pattern. This time you are making up, as well, for other past lifetimes of mistakes. It's all right, friend, but you have to remember your duties. Are you aware of your duties on the planet? Well, duties are: you said to the angels when you were born, that you would help the planet in this time. This is why you came, so we are saying that your duties are to protect the Earth and when you do this you will become more of an able Creator. You are creating on this planet, this moment. So, we are asking you to remember that you have the power to create what you want for yourself. What are you wanting to create? You have to remember, in order to become more of a conscious Creator and thus manifest abundance, you have to step into your abilities. When you are using your abilities to the highest potential, that is when you will be drawing in this abundance because you will be feeling this abundance in your heart and your entire being, you see. When you are remembering who you are and your manifestation power, you will be able to tap into things quite easily. You will not be in this dualistic sense of struggle when you are attempting to perform a job task that is not to your liking. That is quite a slow energy. It is not a creative energy, you see. This is why many artists are loving and creating and feeling abundance because they are tapping into that Divinity which they are, and as you are doing this, that is what will bring you more healing, as well. You see, it is all Divinely timed. That is the positive energy flow that you are wanting so badly because that is who you are. When you tap into who you are, you will be able to manifest more of everything you are wanting tenfold. It constantly increases and increases because you are knowing who you are and when you are remembering who you are, you are showing other people who they are and who they can be. You will be a prime example to other people on this planet. It is quite a beautiful process, seeing the Creators-in-Training on planet Earth, tapping into their Divine potential as human beings, realizing they are Spirit with infinite potential and completely in this energy of Oneness. Oneness Energy is the future and many of you are remembering that it is part of a whole system that is Divinely timed. When you are remembering to focus on that love energy, that is when all the "miracles" are happening. Coincidences? You may notice more of them but we are saying you have the ability to empower other people. You are possibly a coach, you are possibly a communicator. You have many opportunities to fulfill this role you came in with. We are telling you that any kind of work you find, you will be able to move into that space of awakening other people to their own potentials. This is why you are asking us this question, because you yourself are wanting to tap into your innate abilities. We are telling you they are there and you will be able to tap into them. Do you want to know how to do that? Well, you can do that by quieting your mind once in a while. You have noticed some things around you. You may have noticed the time on the clock in an unusual manner. You may have felt this shift in aligned energies. You may feel [that] you resonate with things you did not resonate with before. That is your Higher Self telling you that the energies are now increased in the light quotient. You are noticing things around you. Take note of these things. Focus the light energy and try to remember what was in your childhood that you loved to do. Notice [that] the people around you are reflecting your own personal beliefs. Well, are you wanting to manifest a job? That makes sense, of course it does. You are only human beings, you have nine to five jobs, that is what you all do. We are saying you have the ability to create work for yourself. Have you considered working with the Earth? Have you considered working with the animals of the planet? Have you considered sharing your abilities with elderly people? Many opportunities [are] available to you. You must remember your personal power and you will draw in those experiences that you need to make the next step. You will follow your heart in this succession of events, you see. When your heart is telling you something, that is your soul reminding you of your own abilities. By tapping into your heart, that is what will show you the next step. Many of you are quite intellectual and you want to understand spirituality completely. You want to figure it out like board game or a card game or chess or something like this but life is not exactly like those card games, you see. There are rules, but you can bend the rules because you are a Creator-in-Training. Well, you are quite an ambitious one.

You are wanting to fulfill God's will, yes? We are understanding that you are wanting to fulfill God's mission for you. Well, what we want for you is very simple, but many do not practice [it]: the belief that you are your own God. This is a difficult concept because many of you believe that God is greater and God is better. Well, if you are child of God, you have the seed of God. You are a piece of the entire puzzle. Imagine an ocean wave [and that] you are on that wave. Are you not of the ocean, friend? When we tell you that you are God, many cower, many are afraid: "What does this mean? How big of an ego, you have, Oh Spirit!" Well, we tell you that you are amazing, dear one, and you have such a great power beyond words. We tell the human being of their abilities. Many simply just do not believe it is possible that they are creating everything themselves. It is a hard concept yet very simple and we ask you to remember who you are. The angels are wanting to help you. If we did not care about you, why would we bother with communication? If we were not amazed at your abilities, if we were not ever so grateful for you, why would we come to tell you this? We have no agenda for you, because you are at the end of the line, you see. You are the one who is creating new experiences that God Himself will be experiencing. This is why you are most important at this time. You are on the forefront. You are at the end. You are at the borderline, you see, of the physical dimension. So, when you are remembering who you are, you are doing a service to Tryon. You are doing a service to angels and to God Himself. We speak to you in terms that you are familiar with, but Tryon energy, angelic energy, [is] wanting your happiness. We are wanting your happiness. This is why we come to tell you of your power to create anything you are wanting to create.

ON STARGAZING

When you are stargazing you are focusing energy up and down, through your body. When you are doing this, you are feeling quite content with yourself because you are planting yourself in the ground, if you are outside, and you are also connected to the Universal star systems. There are many, many star systems but your focused intent is what is elevating your energies. When you are focused on these stars, you are bringing in the star knowledge, as well. Can you grasp this? We are communicating to you in a way that cannot be explained with physical words, but it is through the heart, at the moment, and you are feeling this heart-centered energy, right now.

ON PERSONAL DISAPPOINTMENT

This is a lesson at the moment, for many lightworkers. When a person is upset with you, you feel terrible inside because you are focusing this energy inward, of disappointment. You are disappointed in yourselves. How can you be disappointed in yourself when you are doing work of light? When your intention was to help them, your intention was heart-centered and you, to the best of your ability, focused your light on the other one. How could they not feel appreciation? In the grand scheme of things, you see, all is well, and all is coordinated perfectly. It is like an orchestra. If you think one cymbal is out of tune, we would tell you: "It is not out of tune, it is playing a different song." When you are focusing on the melody of one, you are not necessarily seeing the entire picture. You must realize you are helping in the grand scheme of things. This is a very spiritual perspective but it is quite valid. You must have respect for what you are doing because this intention you have is what is most important. We want to remind you of this because it is Spiritual Law that when you have pure intentions, the light will come back to you many times over. You cannot worry about the other one because the other one has their own focus and they are also able to focus the light how they want to. So, if they are venting to you, it is not necessarily your fault. Again, as we said to you before, you are the one listening to them, you are the one helping them. So, when they are complaining, you are doing work just sitting and listening to their woes. We are so sorry not all are ready to commit to making changes in their lives. You see, everyone has their own free will. You know this, dear one, but when the other one is not focusing their light, it feels quite discordant. The energy is not feeling quite aligned and that is why you are disappointed. You see it as a personal failure but we tell you, it is not. You are, dear one, a lightworker. How can you focus this energy on others more, you ask us? Even in times of fear and in feeling that you are not in integrity or not doing enough work, we are telling you, you are doing a tremendously good job and we know you are wanting to see the results. Often, the lightworkers are wanting to see the results in numbers but you are helping tremendously on an energetic level.

FOCUSING ON MANY CLIENTS

It is not only your words, it is your energetic imprint focused through the heart and the light pours through the heart, into the mind of your clients. They are understanding what you truly mean, vibrationally. It is quite hard to explain in physical terms but we reassure you that when the intention is pure, that is when the others are paying you the money, you see. Remember this "place" and a meditation before a session might be quite a good idea to remind you that you are, in essence, doing lightwork, and you are doing a focusing of energy in many different ways in one session. If you are wanting to share this expression of your own light from Home with hundreds or many more, then you certainly can do this. It is more powerful when you are with only one Light Being, but with many, you can call in your angels. You can call in your helpers, the pixies, or whomever you are working with at the moment to help guide many in the audience. You must call in your "gang" so to speak, of helpers. They will help organize these sessions that are more inclined to a larger audience but you must remember your intention. It is something repeated quite frequently but we think you are ready for this and your integrity is quite pure now. It is always good to remember this, and re-remember this in every day of your life. It is not easy all the time, when a negative one, or "a bad apple" tries to ruin it for all, especially with one that is helping but, you see, we are all forgiving on this side of the veil. We see no bad ones. Some do not always remember that they are also of the light, and so they project and they feel that they are failing in life. We tell you, you are simply listening to them. So please, dear one, have compassion for these others and realize you have helped them already tremendously but they are not realizing this in their waking state. Energetically, they are feeling quite better to have had the opportunity to speak with you; it is just [that] they are also wanting the results in a physical form. They are wanting a house, they are wanting a new pony, or they are wanting a yacht, but they are not seeing these things. They are feeling the lack, when in fact, they are constantly working on themselves and growing in new ways. You are helping them with this. Do you believe this, dear one? We believe you are a bit apprehensive sometimes — it is only normal — when in fact you are helping them. It is a fact that we say it is difficult to change in one's self because, when you are forgetting what you have been doing, it is almost as if the ball has been dropped and you are no longer playing the game of life. Sometimes you feel inclined to go back into your hole — just a metaphor there — but, you are feeling that you are wanting to go back into your hole. So the vibrational game-play is not on-going because the other one is not necessarily cooperating. We tell you, no one is to blame but sometimes the energies are not compatible and so, they are not necessarily taking in the advice you have been giving them. We tell you, [that] every time you are coming in with a pure intention , that is what is helping them the most. It is really up to them to make the change in their own lives. You cannot be responsible. We tell you from a recent Kuthumi channeling session [that] has occurred: it is about detaching from the outcome, you see. When another one is playing the game with you and they decide to walk away upset, it is not your fault. You cannot control. You must detach from the outcome. We are not the expert in these emotional games; we are more experts on focusing the light quotients and the Ascension process but we are trying to understand the human emotional system. It is quite complex because it has to do with the thought processes that you are involved with: you are all constantly in flux, constantly changing your thoughts and emotions. Some days you are vibrating very high and some days you are vibrating very low and slowly but it is all for the learning process. So, we know we have not quite touched upon, or given the answer you are seeking. You are wanting to know the mechanics of the corporation and how you can fix this in your physical waking life: "Which papers can I file better?" and "Which phone calls can I make in the morning?" and "Who is the person I should contact in order to have more satisfied customers?" We understand that you are wanting specifics, and we can discuss these but we wanted to tell you your soul's purpose. You must remember that your soul is listening to others and your soul is helping [to] focus light on others through the heart and into the mind. Your soul is wanting a new experience, so anything feeling heavy to you, you must let go like the ball. It should be dropped. In turn, your vibration will go higher. This will also attract more high-vibrational people that will help you construct your business in a fashion that is more to your liking, and to your soul's liking. One big lesson is detachment: detaching from the upset of a client and also detaching from what no longer serves you. These are quite big things in your life. We understand they are not simple and overnight.

ON CRYSTALS

You can connect to many crystals. We think that is a funny joke because you are connecting with many Crystal Children at this time. We think that is the funniest question you have asked us tonight. Obsidian [crystals] will help you with your sibling, to deflect negative energies. We are sorry, but there is much negativity and you can help lift this energy, using a pink energy and obsidian. Perhaps you will give a gift of obsidian to this dear one. You will help her with the pink energy. Just imagine it and ask it to be there. Ask for the Golden Ray to surround her. We are working on it this very moment. As you mentioned crystals, you are already on the way, because you understand that crystals are part of the natural kingdom. This is why you are attracted. Many lightworkers think that the rest of the world is already doing this but we say [that] you are most needed at this time. It is second nature to you that you would work with crystals but, we say, the "joe-shmoe" on the street does not work with crystal energy. We say, hold the light and you will become who you truly already are.

ON EMPATHY

When you have an open heart, you can see into the hearts of others. Sometimes you can even experience what they are experiencing in the present moment. We tell you that, because the present moment is most important. You are not always feeling their past. You think you know they had a heartbreak, but you feel the pain when they are focusing on the pain in the present moment. Do not worry, friend. This is a skill to develop. You can develop your heart chakra even more. The love does not end here. The love extends to many dimensions. The love extends beyond the physical eye and beyond the boundaries of the astral plane. You have the ability to tap into these astral forms of energy. Perhaps you have tried so already. You know when there is energy in your room. You know when some angel is calling you. You know this because you are a powerful Creator.

ADROMEDANS ON DIFFICULT CLIENTS

Andromedans here, Andromedans here. We want to come in and help you with your work. We are coming in on a similar vibration to the Council, but we are Andromedans. Let us have a turn as well, yes? It is a surprise to talk with you. We know you did not expect us. We are Andromedans and we want to tell you "good job" and we are really pleased with what you are doing. You have to keep going. You have to really help these people. They are really needing your help: even this annoying one that is all bugging you and really getting on your nerves. Well, this one is quite an aggressive one, always asking for change, and always asking for results: "When is the money coming in?" They want everything to happen right away, but we tell you, you've got to have patience with them. Even the annoying buggers. You've got to have patience with them because they are really, really needing help the most. They are seeming really, really difficult, but you've got to keep working with those people. We know you want them to go, but they are a big, big lesson. When you help them after that one big struggle, they will really appreciate it more. It's hard to believe, but we have to tell you that [our] coming in to tell you that, means so much to us. We really want to help you. We want you to continue with your work. When you are helping Ascension, even the difficult ones, you're really bringing in more light and we're telling you [that] it is helping the entire universe. We can't tell you how one person makes such a huge impact but that's what you are doing. That's what we wanted to come in and tell you, today. You have guides, you have Andromedan helpers. You can ask us at any time and we will talk to you. We will talk to you. You won't believe that you are — it's like in a meditation. When you're connecting to our energies, we're also connecting to your energy. So, you have to make the conscious choice [of] who you'd like to work with. There are so many of us now, wanting to talk with you and wanting to help you to find the right clients, to find the right mentors. So, we tell you that when you do let go of that one aspect, you are going to attract a different set of clients, you see. They're going to come in, wanting some new tools and you're going to be developing new skills. When you let go of one thing, you're going to be developing a whole new set of skills. It feels really uncomfortable but we're saying you're doing the right thing. When you are helping this really annoying guy — we know who this person is, he's so annoying and he really is not helping you in your day-to-day life, *oh my goodness*, you should just pour him a cup of tea. He's so aggressive and "out there." Don't worry about it because you are helping [him]. Just keep holding the light for [him] and hold a space. You have to look into that — holding an energetic space. You can actually tell him that you're doing that for him. When there's a quiet moment and when all is silent, just tell the person [that] you're holding a space for them. It's like an energetic space, it's like a bubble, for them to release any "guck," or "goo" — that is exactly what this person needs. They need to put a lot of that "yucky stuff" that has been pent up inside in this energetic space. You should also clear your work-space when you're working with this guy, because he's coming in with a lot of "stuff" and he's got to let go of a lot of baggage. What you're doing is, you're helping [him] to heal and release as well. It's quite ironic that often things we are going through *ourselves* is what we're helping others with. It's quite a mirroring activity.

ON HEALING WITH ANGELIC ASSISTANCE

When you are focusing on the angels, you are bringing in their qualities to your life, you see. If you were to focus on an angelic energy in your own energy field, if you were to incorporate the angelic energy into your field, you would be able to use these qualities for the purpose of your exchange. If you are interacting with another one, a like-minded one, you would not need too many words to explain what is happening. You would be able to tap into the angelic quality you are and you would simply know what the other one is thinking about. However, if you are focusing on angelic energy while you are with an "asleep" person, a person who is not awake to their Divinity, then you would be focusing on, perhaps, the opening of their chakra. Perhaps the heart chakra, perhaps the third eye chakra — you would be able to focus on opening a blockage. It is a most important tool of lightworkers. When you are focusing on the healing of blockages of another one, you are doing a service. It is work, friend. It is an energy exchange, of work. You have [the] ability to conduct this kind of work, friend. You have [the] ability to ask the angels to help you with the healing of blockages of other ones. You can do this, friend, we tell you. You have Archangel of the...hold on...old...soul, you are...an Archangel's energy with you, you are an old soul. Angel of Metatron helping you, now. Metatron energy with you. When you are focusing on Metatron Angel [energy], you can heal, [and] help those who want to open their third eye. You also have ability to conduct healing with the angels. Healing with the angels, friend: it is not normal in your society, yet it will become normal. You are an old soul, so you have much experience. You do not have the same limitations as those who are sleeping. Those who are sleeping, need old soul energy to show them that things will work out, you see. Many of the ones asleep fear that they will cease to exist, but you are there to show them that they are safe. You hold the energy for them.

GUIDANCE ON SLEEPING

You have to focus on your Self before you fall asleep, friend, because when you are falling asleep you are needing to connect to your Higher Self. It is a larger part of your soul that is wanting to connect with you, as you are sleeping. As you are transitioning into the sleep period, you must remember to focus on that love that you are, you see. It sounds very common to say this, but when you are focusing on your Higher Self and that connection, it will be quite an easy transition into the sleep state. We know that many of the lightworkers are saying that they have slept so much or too much. It is normal at this time because you are bringing in the Higher Self into the body; this is what is happening. This is why many of you are wanting to take naps during the day. As they say, *siestas*, you know?

ON BELIEFS AND PHYSICAL HEALTH

You are asking of your physical vessel. We are addressing this, now. When you came into the planet, you said you would assist the entire Earth. Much was expected of you but your intention was to do much, as well. You knew that in your healing of others, helping them to heal themselves, would be a reward to your soul. This is one major lesson.

This is why you are enjoying this healing work — it is helping you to heal yourself. This is your path and you are on the right one because you feel the connection to the angels as you are healing. We are teaching that when you focus on the angelic qualities, you become more of the light that you are, you see. There are no physical illnesses. It's an illusion, friend — hard to understand when you are in a physical body. Of course you would say, "Orion, tell me to fix my arm. Tell me to heal my leg." Orion will tell you, "you can heal your own self but it is a lesson." You did not expect it to happen overnight. We now address your entire system of beliefs — most complicated with the human being when you are focusing on the entire system of belief. Do you believe you can heal overnight? This is an act of faith. This is complete faith in God. As a human, you would not jump off of a cliff, dear one. You would be afraid to fall. It is only logical. Similar to asking for God to heal you overnight, your belief system is set up to support your life experience. Perhaps you are feeling ailments in certain parts of the body. We advise you to continue with the healing because it is fine-tuning the parts of your energy field that need to be healed and replaced with other kinds of beliefs, friend. All love you are, but beliefs are what structure this Earthly experience. You know that through your belief system you could transcend the entire human experience but there are aspects of you, also wanting to focus on the physical world. You are also catering to these physical aspects that are expressing themselves, now. Many aspects and new ones have come in, because the lightworker asked for Divine Intervention, you see. What a beautiful game. When [a] lightworker asks for angels and help, you change the entire game, friends. This is all of your doing. Our joke, but it is truth because you asked for angels and angels came to the planet. You can ask for more, and more and more. This is the beauty of the game. You still want to influence life on planet Earth, but you [also] still want to transcend life on planet Earth. You still want to heal parts of your energy field before you transcend Earth. You also wanted to help those who came before you. You wanted to help the planet. So we say, what is your goal, friends? Are you focusing on the healing of your field, are you focusing on the healing of the planet, or your client? So many ways to focus, so little time, it seems. We advise that you focus on what you feel needs to be focused on most. This is our guidance to you. When you know something needs attention and you feel it in your heart, that is a sign for you to go in that direction. So many focus on the mind. Illusion says that the mind will transcend ego, but the mind is also controlled by many aspects of the ego. [Many also focus on the mind as] a way to transcend life, however it is a difficult one because of all the beliefs humanity holds, and the mass consciousness as well. You will be shown the way; it is the way of the heart.

ON RELATIONSHIPS

Yes, friend. We are witnessing many lightworkers asking the same question, Krista says. "Why does my partner not listen to me discuss the Spirit World? Why is so difficult to communicate sometimes?" We understand. There is a love here, there is a love on the planet Earth, now. Many of you are connected to this love through your hearts. You have helped those who are not connected, to connect. Once you made the connection you asked, "What next for us? We are still together, we are still connected in the heart." Then you wonder why things are not getting better. We say the healing has happened. The service has been done. Many of you are sitting in the same pool and saying you want to splash around, but something is holding you back. So many lightworkers are wanting to expand. In your society, relationships are not always allowing this expansion to occur. You are having these rules when you are in relationships. When you are heart-centered with another being, you tell each other, "Do not look to the other one for love. Do not look to them," but still your heart is looking to them for love. You perhaps have witnessed the love of other ones. This is quite normal and it is all right. Do not worry, friend. You are not breaking any rules. Your loved ones will always love you no matter what, you know this, but when you are in this new energy you will love so many more. You will wonder why you are focusing on these new ones who are so beautiful and you will start to ask yourself, "Am I wrong?" We say, your loved one has not disappeared. You helped your loved one, in many ways. Your loved one is now focusing in a new way because of your help. We do not ask your society to change its rules. Your society has rules because the system depends on them. This is why you either shift within the system or you try to change the system. It is always up to you and your relationship with your partner. Do you realize [that] in any moment you have an option? Perhaps focusing on the option that you have, will give you much more peace of mind. Focus on the fact that you have the ability to choose in any moment, friend. You can choose in any moment. Freedom is what will help you, now. You can stay or you will go, but you will always have love there. We do not tell you to remove someone from your life, because it is not true but you can choose to associate and to spend more time with another one. Your time is precious on this Earth and you are doing most valuable work at this time. Who are you wanting to spend time with, dear one? The answers come when you look at the other one. What do you see when you look into their space? Do you see happiness, do you see tears? What are you seeing when you focus on them? Perhaps they reflect back to you a part of yourself that you left behind. Perhaps you say, "I am no longer this way. I am no longer a sad, sad, person. I am a happy person, now." Perhaps you look at your old friends and you say, "You show me how things used to be but they are not like this anymore. We can move forward together, or we can change our relationship, or we cannot change our relationship." You must discuss with your friend what you are wanting, but we say that it is always up to you. You are the one that is in control. Perhaps you want to feel more free. We say, do not limit your freedom whatsoever. You have the freedom at all times. You are worried, as a wonderful woman, if you will upset the other one. This is a constant concern: "I want to keep the peace. I am a lightworker. I must focus on the love," but we say, it is always there. It is not selfish to love yourself. Big lesson for many lightworkers: to love the self is not selfish — that is a belief that has been taught to you by your society. "I am beautiful," you say. The other one says, "You are full of it! You cannot say that about yourself!" but it is true that you are beautiful, you are love, you are perfect. Many say you are not. We also want to address the fact that the new energies here are changing the dynamics for many males and females. In this new light quotient coming in, there are many, many males, who are connecting to their feminine aspects, more so than before. Also, many females [are] connecting to their feminine aspects. No longer are these females nurturing the other one; they are nurturing the Self. They say, "Finally, I learn that in this new energy, I can love myself

322

freely. I deserve this love energy. Before, I was told that I must constantly give unto others and give of myself unto others." To love the Self: it is key in every situation. We are giving you an example, yes? A practice example. When you walk into the room, before you open the door to your loved one, perhaps you will first focus your energy before you open the door to them. Perhaps you will say to yourself, "I want to focus this light first within me." When you are in your escalator, when you are in your car, first, before you go on your dates, remember to focus the light within yourself. Focus on how much you love yourself. Focus on your own beauty, first. Then, when you open the door you will shine your beauty unto the other one and you will say, "I love myself no matter what you say to me!" And the other one might look at you, and they might not understand what you are doing with your energy. They will say, "Stop that energy! I am the one in control." That is not fair. You must focus the light within yourself, first. It is something we constantly repeat because it is true and it is necessary in Ascension. Before you make a decision, focus the light within yourself. We say that most of the discomfort human beings are experiencing is the discomfort when they are not making a decision. Not making a decision causes a stressful energy. It is not moving. You must keep the flow of energy moving. You must constantly flow your energy. This is why we advise you to focus on the modalities as we said before: in your New Age you have many tools. You have yogas. You have ways of breathing. When you focus on these things, you will be flowing the energy out. It will not be in the same place. Just as you change your wardrobes, friend, just as you wash your makeups, just as you change your cars, you are constantly keeping energy moving. This is why you do not sit on a pile of cash. You want to keep the energy moving and the economy flowing. We say the same is with your relationships, as well. You want the flow to happen. When you are in a place of indecision, this is when you experience stressful patterns. They are not beneficial. You must make the choice first, friend.

ON BEING SELFISH

We know this is quite an uncomfortable statement but most of the time, when the lightworker is wanting to create, it is quite often a selfish act — a good one. We say "selfish" because it is always about you. It is always about the lightworker's own soul growth or evolution, as you say. We say, when you create, you are creating because it is something you need. Many at this time, need to discuss spirituality because they need to believe in it themselves. [Just] as you have a doctor who wants to be a doctor, [it is] often because they need to heal themselves. Don't you love how the system works? Everyone wins, you see. It is a perfect system of creation. Everyone wins. When you bring in more of your light, you are bringing in more light into this entire system and it stays in the system, friend. We know the laws of energy. We know the New Age discusses the old way of life falling away. We know it feels like something is leaving but that is because something new is coming.

ANGELS ON DISCORDANT VIBRATIONS

Hello, friend; angels here. You have to remember that with an illness or any discordant vibration, you feel as if you did not deserve it and you ask why you have to witness this kind of experience. "What did I do? Was it a past-life karma? Am I being punished?" Typical beliefs or questions — not all voiced but still felt in the heart. "Why did I suffer this?" The muscular system is what holds everything together. How are you feeling when things seem to fall apart in your life? You may feel it in your entire body, friend. You will feel discordant energies because it is happening around you. You feel it to the very core of your Self. [The] muscular system is holding everything together. Have you had to be the one to do this with others? Please, friend, realize, [a] muscle also needs to relax; [a] muscle also needs to rejuvenate itself. Perhaps you feel that the problem is in another part of the body, but much of the support system in your body is reflecting to you what you are experiencing in your life. Angels here to tell you this. Please remember, what you see outside of yourself is a reflection of what is going on inside. As above, so below, friend. Please do not be cross with us, we know that you can feel annoyed: "I do not deserve this experience for myself. I have served God my whole life. Why me?" But we show you, you are a Creator. Next lesson for you, friend [is] to realize, your creative ability — not the artistic side, this you are, but the creative Self that has summoned experiences in order for your soul to reach a new level of being. When you are focusing on the pain, you will experience pain. We understand it is not simple, that you [can] just take a pill and it all goes away. We understand the underlying causes of these malfunctions. "Why do I have this? It must be a past life." Well, friend, we say it is reflecting back to you what you are seeing around you. How is a family held together? How is the community around me? Who makes sure everyone is satisfied? Who makes sure everyone has support? What is it saying to you, friend, [this] muscular system holding everything together? We repeat: [the] muscular system [is] holding everything together. Many of [the] lightworkers now, have a huge lesson to learn; not only yourself. Many other ones are realizing that they have a spiritual support system available. It is a huge lesson for all at this time. You have evidence of it in your daily lives. This is why you are interested in the angels. This is why you are interested in the psychics, because you say, "How did she know that about me? She's a psychic one!" and many are reading the occultic texts. These are simply proof that you have a spiritual support system, holding everything together. Trusting in the universe is a big lesson, friend. When you feel you are not the one to hold everything together, we tell you, you will release much of your pain but you will have to find who holds everything together. Who is the "spinal cord" of the Earth? Who is the "muscular system" of the Earth? You may want to experience a new location as well, friend. Much of your pain is because you have had a hard time in your home environment, dear one. We say, you must remember that you have a spiritual support system and the trusting that you do is a major lesson of so many at this time. We wish for your happiness and we wish to discuss happiness with you. We understand that pain is part of the human experience but we say that when you focus on the pain it creates more of it. This is why we would rather focus on the support that is available to you, friend. A healing [is] happening when you focus on your support. Who is supporting you? How do you have support from Spirit? "Which entities are supporting me now?" This will help you release your pain, when you truly remove the belief you are not supported enough. Then, you will be able to focus more light within your skeletal-muscular systems, friend. We hope this enlightened your question somewhat. Hopefully it made sense. Please understand, you have support at all times. You must ask the angels.

ANDROMEDANS ON TECHNOLOGY AND MUSIC

Hello friend, how are you? Hello, hello, hello. We are here to discuss anything you would like to discuss, but first we want to tell you how happy we are to talk to you. Andromedans here for your Ascension, as well. Andromedans are also wanting to talk about the technologies. You have many, many technologies in your system but they are not quite up-to-date. Andromedans are wanting to help you fine-tune the science that exists on your plane. We have many in the stars now, working with your science. Your scientists are tuning into our thoughts, tuning into our thought-patterns. Your scientists are wanting to awaken themselves. How can they incorporate their dreams into their actual work? Many of your scientists now, are starting to have dreams they cannot explain. They wake up one morning and they say, "Oh, my goodness! I solved the riddle of my conundulumdulum [conundrum]" and then they realize that this answer came from their dream-space. They wonder what is going on and your quantum physicists are now tapping into this infinite potential of the photon energy. How exciting that is, friend! Andromedans are wanting to help you, as well. We have many, many fleets, starfleets. Of course, we do, we are Andromedans! Who else would have a starfleet? We are focusing on your sciences, now. We are also wanting to talk about the planetary systems that exist in your solar system. Many of us are etheric, yes, you could say that, but we also have our focus in physicality as well. Many will not be able to relate to us because we tend to focus in and out of this physical existence. We are even able to take on human form but our "outfit" is not quite as refined as the real human being is. We have many here, wanting to discuss science with you however another vessel will be needed; Krista is not proficient in the sciences. We want to tell others that it is possible to communicate with Andromeda. Andromedans are your friends. Andromedans are here for Ascension as well, also wanting to help you with your energy. You are all wanting to tap into a new form of energy. We are not allowed to share all of our secrets with you because it would disrupt the process of your own evolution. How would your society have pride in itself if we were to tell you how to have an Andromedan spaceship? You would no longer have a similar human experience, you would have an Andromedan experience and that is not fair to you. We are wanting to behave in a brotherly fashion. It is our duty. Your music is quite fascinating, friend. Have you noticed the symbols when you are writing your music? Have you noticed the patterns of the symbols when you are writing your music? You are writing different wavelengths. You understand that waves come and go. You understand that the brain works in wavelengths. So does your music. Do you realize they relate to each other when you synchronize the brain waves with musical notes? How exciting, friend! We want to tell you that you can affect the music just as you can affect the brain and vice versa, both are affecting the other one. You can do this, friend. You can also pattern your instruments in a way that can create a symphony that will sound like... well, many of your friends of the light. We are on a different wavelength, now. You are feeling our energy. It's very fast, but we are wanting to talk about your music. Your music has a fascinating quality to help some of those in need. Please focus on the patterns on the sheet you are creating. Remember that a brainwave has its ups and down, but you can affect the brainwave with your music. Have you looked into this, friend? There are many of you on the planet now, who are tapping into this potential healing with music. It is something that people are doing every day of their lives. They play their favorite songs because they know their favorite songs are healing them. It's a quite obvious statement, but we want to say to you [that] we want you to focus on the binary waves, binary frequencies. We also want you to focus on the light, photon light. It is another interest of Andromedan energy; the photon energy. Many are also incorporating the photon energy in their healing practices. When you incorporate these two, you have a very powerful mode of healing. When you work with the light to create your music, sometimes you will just experience a flow. If you want to connect with your friends in Andromeda, you simply have to ask us to download music. You will possibly hear etheric music as you are falling asleep. This is because your brainwaves are synchronizing with the higher vibration. As you are falling asleep, you will tend to hear patterns, you will tend to hear sounds. You may want to be creative just upon waking, friend. This is how you will remember. Remember the binary patterns. So many of us are wanting to talk to you, friend. Please invite us into your energy field. We have respect for you, so we tell you and we guide you to shield yourself from the other energies around. We will not disrupt you but if you invite us in, we would like to work on your noticing of the musical patterns on your sheets. Ask us, invite us in, and we will help you download new ideas for your writing of this music. Please, we ask you to enjoy the process, because when you do, it is more fun for us. So, when you are focusing on your musical abilities, remember, you are also synchronizing your brainwaves with the music you are playing.

ON HELPING IN THE DREAM-SPACE

[In your dream-space] yes, you are helping those who pass over. Before, you have been an angel helping those to pass on. It was part of your training in preparation for your physical life. You are an expert at helping others to pass on into the light. Sometimes you tend to do this as you sleep however you are also focused on the Earth, the natural Earth. We are sending you much-needed energy at the moment.

ANSWERS HIDDEN IN NUMBERS

[Birthdates] are the vibrations you came in with. Are you aware of the meaning behind 1 and 8? 1 is Creator [and] 8 is the infinity symbol. You see it as a number sequence. What you are seeing is 18. Much can be decoded from one and two numbers. Together, they have a different vibration. Just as you feel differently with other friends, you have a joint energy with the two energies. Do you understand, friend? 1 and 8 create a different energy, not separate but a different energy. You can have 1 alone and 8 alone and together they create a new energy, friend — a combination. The Creator is 1. The first and foremost number 1, it means "Oneness." It is the beginning. It is All That Was and All That Will Be, All-That-Is. That is the meaning of [number] 1. [Number] 8 is infinity. It is also a sacred geometry or energy [that] flows in a figure 8 sometimes — it is continuity. [Together, 1+8 means] that you continue to bring in the energy of Creator. You have this number in your life because you have appeared here before and it is reminding you of your life mission, friend.

Are you interested in knowing your life mission? Well, we are humorous. We know you are a curious one and so we would like to help you with your questions. A life mission is something you knew before you came in, something you already know and something you can access in your sleep space — the 18 energies. Orion wants to say that the 18 holds much. It holds the keys to the Ascension program. [It] holds the key to messages in the dream-space. [It] holds meaning to the... hard to say... *space-in-between-the-space* — hard to explain in physical terms. You have the physical space and you have an etheric realm surrounding the physical space. What is in between is the 18 energy; [it] is what brings these two layers together. You could research the history behind this number. You would intuitively perceive what is correct, what is truth. You would feel it in your heart-space. You are wondering now, what is the *space-in-between-space*. If you [are to] have continuity in life, you need form to give direction to this Infinite Source of Energy. Form must be given to Infinite Energy that is rampant and unorganized. The 18 solidifies etheric energy with the physical energy. It can withstand Creative Life-Force Energy as well as the etheric film that surrounds the physical layer. Friend, we understand it is not easy to grasp. As a physical being, you have many layers to your Essence. This number is reminding you of the fact that you are a channel. Your body holds a certain structure and the 8 is the energy flowing into your form. You must imagine the body as a capsule. Perhaps the 1 is like a canal, or a channel or a cord or a tube or two straight lines or perhaps a straight line, and within the straight line you have a figure 8. It is energy flowing. Perhaps you are familiar with energy currents, friend. Imagine you are wanting to transmit energy flow, radiowaves perhaps, or color sequences —

light. It must reflect in a zigzag energy if you had light and pyramids and crystals and so on. We explain that the 8 is like an electric current and the 1 is what is holding the current within itself. Hard to grasp, but what we are getting at is that as a channel, you conduct the Energy of Life, Creative Life Force. You channel Creative Life Force. It is in your makeup, it is in your astrological chart, it is. The answers are hidden in the numbers, friend. Many human beings are wanting to create labels for things. We have trouble with Krista because she is always asking us for labels for everything that occurs. In the Kingdom of Heaven there are no labels — everything simply "is," but we understand there is a need to know why specific events are occurring, so we will give you a few answers that will ease your mind. [For example, you are seeing 11:11, 333, 444, 555, repeating.] The sequence of ones are for new beginnings. It was an agreement for the Collective Consciousness to see these numbers. It is subtle and it is something that science cannot disregard. Science cannot disregard the fact that human beings are having synchronicities; it is a subtle event. The ones are beginning a New Age for humanity — quite [an] obvious answer. Your birthdate is significant. [It] is what you chose [on] the day you chose to come into this world — you chose it before you were born, friend. You asked why the 1 and 8? We have answered the vibrations of the numbers. We have answered that the 1 signifies new beginnings. Your soul is wanting to reprogram the course it was going to take, to begin a new course. It wants to take action now, and your soul wants you to be healed and to deliver messages from the Divine, as well as wake you up to all of your Divine gifts. That is why you are seeing the numbers, dear one. You are being reminded of your gifts and this is why you are attracted to these modalities. Subtle signs.

333

Spirit is subtle. Spirit is not here to scare you because it is who you are. Spirit respects who you are.

ON STARSEEDS

Starseeds are beautiful creatures. Many feel as if they are not of the Earth, when in fact, many of them are of the Earth. The Earth is an old place and many starseeds have helped to create life on Earth; many set up this entire system. They do not even recall. Many of the starseeds are now enjoying physical reality, [yet] many are coming [here] temporarily [and] many are wanting to leave this "horrific" place. They do not like Earth, oh goodness! They think the Earth is polluted and full of "meanies" but we say that starseeds are here to help. Starseeds are not living such difficult lives because they are helpers, you see. They do not have the karmic lessons to learn. We say, simply being a starseed does not mean you have the easy way out, it does not mean anyone is better than anyone else. [It] simply means that you have history in other star systems.

ON WORKING WITH CHILDREN

Your gift is to focus the energy of the little ones. They have too much energy, sometimes. You have to help the little ones calm down; this energy must be focused in a new way. You have this whole system of tools available to you. When you realize that this system is to help you spread the light, you will be grateful for all information you receive. We guide you to help the ones with too much energy. It is not focused energy. When they focus the energy, change is made on the planet. When it is frazzled energy, it does no good for others. The classroom sometimes focuses the artwork [which] helps them to focus. Do you realize [that] when the children are completing art projects and drawing, they are often very quiet? When they are making music, they are very loud, however the focus is key. You can show them that to play an instrument is a skill. You do not simply place your hands upon the instrument. You can show them [that] they need to have a certain stance when they play these instruments. You can show them [that] they need to hold up their arms and they need to listen to the fine sounds of the instruments. One thing at a time, for the little ones. They are all over the place because their parents, as well, [are] asking them to focus everywhere. They are being asked to become these perfect citizens but they are so little. They cannot worry about so many things. When they are focused on one thing at a time and they become proficient at one instrument, they will feel tremendous satisfaction within themselves, because they were able to master something in such a short time. We advise you to begin with a smaller and simple instrument first. Do not hand a piano to a three-year-old. This is just a silly example, but it is quite important. You would not give a huge toy to a tiny little baby. You would start out with something simple and then you would expand on that one. When you ask the little ones to focus their energy, you are not using your words. When you are focusing on the energies of the little ones, you must show them how intricate one instrument is. You must be excited about the instrument and all of its aspects. This is also helping you fine-tune your own musical abilities. When you create that music, you will be able to create something quite specific. That is quite a science, friend. Do you realize that [there] is a science behind writing the music? The entire fact that you hear a note, and it is processed by the whole neurological system, is an interesting development. Perhaps you would like to teach about how the music affects the brain. Which child is not interested in the juicy guts of the brain? This, perhaps, is an interesting lesson. Perhaps you will be one of those who brings in more interesting experiences to the school system. Perhaps the school systems are changing. We simply pose this idea because many are not satisfied with the old school system — so many rules. Of course, [the] intention was to help the little ones focus. Perhaps they can express parts of themselves through one instrument. You can explain the dynamics of the instrument and what it does to the brain and to the energy field. Perhaps you will begin projects where you are focusing your love on the little ones as well as the music, and you will ask them: "How does this song make you feel?" You will ask them questions their parents have not asked them before. You can ask them: "What does this song remind you of?" You can ask the little ones to contribute to the lesson. Do you think that a teacher is the only one teaching? No, that is backwards in your society. Do you think that when there is interaction, it is only in one direction? Do you think you are the one in control always? Of course, in your society, the older ones are always having control, however we say that it is not always up to the teacher to control the class. Quite shocking, is it not, friend? Have you accepted the fact that you can heal with your music, friend? Have you noticed the calming energies when you are working with the little ones — how they are calmer with your songs? Have you noticed that? The world is needing of more light and more light-filled music, not enough music with light in it. Many will be helped by your beautiful songs. Have you created music for others as well, friend? You will energize your own vibration when you focus the light on your music. "How can I serve the little energetic ones? Perhaps I will create something they can use in their homes. Perhaps I will create something others can listen to, as well." You have this ability — you can ask the angels to work with you when you write a song. You can create healing music. You can create sounds of the angels with your instruments or your singing ability. Have you tried this, friend? You can do it, friend. Not to worry, friend. So many opportunities. You are a bright light. How do you want to shine it? It is up to you. Perhaps we have posed these ideas because they are something your soul perhaps wants to do. In this new energy, new aspects are becoming more involved in your daily lives. This is why many lightworkers are asking what is happening. The new energy is changing the old system and self expression in the new system is necessary in this new energy, you see. Many of you would say the Age of Aquarius is about the expression of the individuality. So, if your aspect is self-expression, wanting to express itself as a particle of the soul, now coming to the surface of the new energy, we say, you can incorporate it in your lesson, or you can incorporate it inside of the classroom. Either way, either case, the aspect will want to express itself. This is our advice. You can take it how you want to. Now, the writing process is an interesting one. Many are opening their psychic abilities through writing. They are saying words that resonate with the people they interact with. All the words are vibrations as well, that also carry their own meaning. If you are wanting self-expression with the writing, that will fulfill one aspect. However, if you are wanting to heal with writing, that is a healing aspect. Writing is the avenue of expression. If you are wanting to write, you must know what the aspect is wanting to be expressed. You must tap into what you intend to do, you see. You understand, yes? When you are intentionally creating, that is when the writing becomes powerful. If you are wanting to heal yourself, perhaps you will not distribute that in the newspapers. We are saying that writing is one avenue.

ON ELVES

We guide and say [that] you are multi-dimensional and you are focused in many places at once. You are from a blue planet, friend. You have a connection with the Deva Kingdom and to the Elven energies. The Elven race is the Deva aspect of yourself. You have parts of your being that are involved with the natural kingdom because you are more than what you see in the mirror, dear one. You are focused in the physical as well as the natural kingdom, therefore you could call yourself part Elven, but we say your soul is from the Blue Planet, Blue Ray of Creation, Blue Ray children. You are focused in this lifetime however, on the ancient civilizations of the Earth, because you are learning what to bring into this life experience. As your soul is focused in ancient cultures, you are able to facilitate what is needed in this moment. You are working with the Golden Energies in this lifetime. Many of the ones who live on Earth are wanting to revive the planet and nature. You are recalling the signs. You are recalling your Divine Mission. The things [that] you are wanting most are reminding you of what you wanted to accomplish here. The Ascension program now is allowing many to fulfill their missions and the Blue Energy holds much information on reviving the planet. You can help Earth breathe again.

ON OPENING TO CHANNEL

In order to bring in, you must ask who you want to bring in, friend. Much fear is involved in the transition to opening yourself. If you were to open, you would perhaps be in contact with many Spirits — we say, "Earth-bound entities." Those are the ones that cause the most trouble to many. We do not disregard them because they simply need help. When you bring in the light energies, you are able to clear the space. You can decide whom you want to connect with. When you are open, you must become a reader of others' energies and you must also clear your own space and your own body. You must work with the benevolent energies if you want to communicate and channel the benevolent energies. Many are able to connect with the astral layer; that is where you go after you fall asleep. It is something you would, perhaps, want guidance with. We say that when you work with the astral, much what appears to be "magic" happens. We do not discuss magic, however there are many who have become proficient in working with the alchemy of the physical and the astral. There are many energies everywhere and many layers. You experience time and space but it is not existing in the other layers, you see. You think that you are alone at all times and you think that you are one solid mass of energy. Well, you are much, much more and you are interacting with many layers of existence at once. When you experience movements or energies, they are often your own. Need not worry friend, however do be aware that you will become an energy reader if you begin to channel. If you are wanting to channel-spoken, you can do so.

ON RAISING YOUR VIBRATION

That is a very good question, friend, because you are saying that you are realizing more of your soul is being incorporated into your body at this moment. When you set the energy through your chakras at night, you are able to transcend the body, but when you are asking in your waking state, to bring the soul into the body, you are doing a tremendous act. Do you see, dear one, how the energy system is balanced? You have been used to an energy system in your body your entire life. Now, you are asking for more of your soul to be incorporated into your body. When this happens, the energy of your entire bodily system shifts. We say that if you were to incorporate the entire soul into your body, it would stop working. It would stop working because it is too much light. You can only hold so much light, now. Especially for those of you that are helpers, we do not allow too much light into the body. It is controlled, because too much light in your body would disrupt, and who would fulfill your task as the way-shower to others? When you are living in love, this is a service to All-That-Is. When you walk into a room, and you hold open your arms in love and show everyone with your energy that you love them, you are doing a tremendous act of service. This is what is bringing more light to every situation. We do not want to burden you, because there are so many ways you can focus your light. You can focus your light on objects as well as living beings. We have said before [that] Gaia needs your help, now. Gaia was feeling restless energy and not sure to erupt certain volcanoes. Gaia decided that the shift in the ocean would be better. This is why many human beings felt much fluctuation in the emotions, lately. Yesterday was a big day for many lightworkers because of the emotional changes. (11/2011) The more open you are to your soul, [the] more energy steps into your body. Every time you focus the light, the more light you become. When your waking self walks around with this hat on that says "I am of the light," that is what brings in more light. It is a challenge because every lightworker gets distracted. Every lightworker must focus on light and physical reality. If you are able to fill the oil in your car and you are able to focus the light, this is a lesson learned. It is something you must practice over and over, until you are able to hold that new light quotient in. So often, lightworkers forget about the light because they are distracted by negative energy. We say, do not worry about the negative energies but when you encounter them, this is when you will be tested and you will [be] asked of for service: to use your light quotient. Many times, the lightworker will fill themselves to the brim, go out in the world, and feel depleted after an act of service. This only means that you need to refill your cup. In past lifetimes, you have been a depleted lightworker. In the past lives, you have had opportunities to replenish your cup, and now you are also asking us for permission, as well. We are your friends and we tell you, you must replenish your own cup. In the past, many lightworkers were not available to the masses. In your day and age, you have a new avenue that connects everyone. Of course, you know what it is — it is the Internet. In the past, you were a lightworker but you did not have the same contact to so many people. This is why we say the opportunities are endless. You have day-to-day interaction as well as Internet interaction.

AFTERWORD

Creation is happening on all levels. The Orion Council says that when we consciously intend to create with Creator's light, we are en-lightened -that is, we are given more light in the form of information, healing, love, or whatever else we desire. We have all chosen to be born into the third dimension to experience what is furthest from Creator and then return Home again.

As my work expands, so my perception of healing, love, angelic realms, groups of consciousness, interdimensional beings and layers of reality expands. In the higher (but not better) dimensions, I find that we can crack codes, receive adjustments to our light bodies, and learn to ask better questions of Creator. The Council confirms that recipients of channeled messages are experiencing much more than words. My clients are now "downloading" templates for creative projects and Andromedan symbols, which will be the subject of a future book.

We are living in the most exciting time in existence: let us accept our endless opportunities for expansion, experience and expression. All energy is love and we are magnificent, sovereign Beings of Light, evolving in love, into eternity.

19373787R00198

Made in the USA
San Bernardino, CA
23 February 2015